GRACE IN THE WILDERNESS

—

*A STUDY ON
THE BOOK OF 1 PETER*

KRISTIN SCHMUCKER

STUDY SUGGESTIONS

Thank you for choosing this study to help you dig into God's Word. We are so passionate about women getting into Scripture, and we are praying that this study will be a tool to help you do that. Here are a few tips to help you get the most from this study:

- Before you begin, take time to look into the context of the book. Find out who wrote it, and learn about the cultural climate it was written in, as well as where it fits on the biblical timeline. Then take time to read through the entire book of the Bible we are studying if you are able. This will help you to get the big picture of the book and will aid in comprehension, interpretation, and application.

- Start your study time with prayer. Ask God to help you understand what you are reading, and allow it to transform you (Psalm 119:18).

- Look into the context of the book as well as the specific passage.

- Before reading what is written in the study, read the assigned passage! Repetitive reading is one of the best ways to study God's Word. Read it several times, if you are able, before going on to the study. Read in several translations if you find it helpful.

- As you read the text, mark down observations and questions. Write down things that stand out to you, things that you notice, or things that you don't understand. Look up important words in a dictionary or interlinear Bible.

- Look for things like verbs, commands, and references to God. Notice key terms and themes throughout the passage.

- After you have worked through the text, read what is written in the study. Take time to look up any cross-references mentioned as you study.

- Then work through the questions provided in the book. Read and answer them prayerfully.

- Paraphrase or summarize the passage, or even just one verse from the passage. Putting it into your own words helps you to slow down and think through every word.

- Focus your heart on the character of God that you have seen in this passage. What do you learn about God from the passage you have studied? Adore Him, and praise Him for who He is.

- Think and pray through application and how this passage should change you. Get specific with yourself. Resist the urge to apply the passage to others. Do you have sin to confess? How should this passage impact your attitude toward people or circumstances? Does the passage command you to do something? Do you need to trust Him for something in your life? How does the truth of the gospel impact your everyday life?

- We recommend you have a Bible, pen, highlighters, and journal as you work through this study. We recommend that ballpoint pens instead of gel pens be used in the study book to prevent smearing.

Here are several other optional resources that you may find helpful as you study:

- www.blueletterbible.org This free website is a great resource for digging deeper. You can find translation comparison, an interlinear option to look at words in the original languages, Bible dictionaries, and even commentary.

- A dictionary. If looking up words in the Hebrew and Greek feels intimidating, look up words in English. Often times we assume we know the meaning of a word, but looking it up and seeing its definition can help us understand a passage better.

- A double-spaced copy of the text. You can use a website like www.biblegateway.com to copy the text of a passage and print out a double-spaced copy to be able to mark on easily. Circle, underline, highlight, draw arrows, and mark in any way you would like to help you dig deeper and work through a passage.

TABLE OF CONTENTS

—

GOSPEL-
HOPE
—

WEEK 1 | DAY 1

Read
1 PETER

Gospel-hope. That is what the book of 1 Peter is all about. The author of the book is the Apostle Peter, and the book was written at the end of his life. Peter was a disciple of Jesus, and many have been fascinated with his story and the relatability of this imperfect disciple. Peter was a fisherman who was called to be a disciple of Jesus (Matthew 4:18-20). He was a brave and bold follower of Christ known also for his impulsive behavior and even his failures. In the Gospels we see Peter as a man struggling forward. He is a close follower and friend of Jesus, and yet he struggles to trust. He is the disciple who walked on water with Jesus though he began to sink as he took his eyes off of Jesus (Matthew 14:28-31). He was corrected by Jesus (Matthew 16:23). He fell asleep after Jesus had called the disciples to pray in Gethsemane (Matthew 26:36-46), and then he cut off the ear of one of the soldiers coming to arrest Jesus (Matthew 26:51-52). And at the time of Jesus' crucifixion, he denied Jesus three times just as Jesus had told him he would do (Matthew 26:69-75).

Yet despite his many failings, Peter was a passionate follower of Jesus. He is one of the disciples believed to be in the inner circle of Jesus. He beautifully declared Jesus to be the Messiah, and Jesus would tell Peter that he would be a great leader in the church (Matthew 16:13-20). After Jesus' resurrection and Peter's denial of Christ there is a poignant scene where Jesus calls Peter to repentance and asks Peter to declare his love for Christ. Though Peter had denied Jesus three times, we see Peter now declare his love for Jesus three times as Jesus commends him to feed His sheep (John 21). The leadership in the church that Jesus had promised to Peter is clearly seen after the resurrection in the book of Acts. We see Peter preach with power in Acts 2 and serve and lead the church through the entire book of Acts. Peter was a man changed by the grace of God and the truth of the resurrection. He went from a stumbling disciple to one of the most influential apostles in the early church. Perhaps this is why we love Peter so much. We see ourselves in his moments of weakness and pray that God in His grace will choose to use us to build His kingdom despite our many failures. Peter is a testament to the grace of God as is every believer who has been transformed by the hope of the gospel.

The book of 1 Peter was written by the Apostle Peter to Christians in the areas of Pontus, Galatia, Cappadocia, Asia, and Bithynia which are located in Asia Minor. The book likely written from Rome, is thought by most scholars to have been written between A.D. 60-68 during the

reign of Nero and his brutal persecution of the Christian church in Rome. Church tradition tells us that Peter was crucified upside down in A.D. 68, and most believe that it would have been written before A.D. 65 which is when a great fire was set in Rome. The fire was assumed to have been set by Nero and blamed on Christians, resulting in an even greater level of persecution. 1 Peter would be the encouragement that these believers needed to fix their eyes on Jesus and the example that He gave as they endured and even were martyred for their belief in Jesus.

The book is an encouraging letter from Peter to those believers and contains themes of God's grace, the suffering of Jesus and believers, the hope of the gospel, as well as life in a world that is not our home. 1 Peter is rich with deep, theological truth that propels us to live the Christian life with purpose and conviction. It calls us to look to Jesus. It calls us to live in His example. It reminds us of the hope that is found in the gospel. It calls us to holiness. It reminds us of who we are and how we should live. It calls us to stand firm in the grace that has been given to us.

———

Perhaps this is why we love Peter so much.

We see ourselves in his moments of weakness and pray that God in His grace will choose to use us to build His kingdom despite our many failures.

As you have read through 1 Peter, write down the key themes that you identify in the book.

After reading through 1 Peter, summarize the message of the book.

Look up some of the verses from today's study about Peter.
In what ways do you identify with Peter?

Chosen Exiles

WEEK 1 | DAY 2

Read
1 PETER 1:1-2

As we begin to dig into the book of 1 Peter, we see the richness of the gospel even just in the first verse. We are being reminded of who we are and of all that God has done for His children. Peter begins the letter in humility, speaking more of his audience than of himself. He addresses the letter to the elect or chosen exiles, and these first words give us great insight into the message of the book of 1 Peter. As God's people, we are set apart for obedience. We are chosen and elect by God, and we are also exiles, strangers, and aliens in this world that we live in. This world is not our home. We live for a kingdom that is not of this earth. Exiles of the dispersion, or those dispersed abroad, are literally of the diaspora. This language is drawing our memories back to the dispersion of God's people during the exile of the Old Testament. The concept of God's people as wanderers is not a new concept in Scripture. From the calling of Abraham in the book of Genesis, to the wanderings in the wilderness of the Hebrew people, to the dispersion and exile of Israel—God's people are a people of the wilderness. The church is no different. In Peter's day they were spread throughout the known world, and today the church is spread across the earth. We are exiles because this is not our country. We wander in the wilderness of this world as exiles longing for our true home and living for our Savior right where we have found ourselves. And we find grace in the wilderness.

Sometimes it seems that we are shocked by the fact that we are exiles and strangers. We marvel at the depravity of our world and forget that we were never meant to fit into the crowd. He did not only foreknow us as His people, but He also foreknew our circumstances. He has called us as His children, and He has called us to the exact circumstances of the life we are living. God is not surprised by our sufferings or our wanderings. He has chosen us as His people, and He has chosen us for this moment. In His providence, He has placed us here just as He did Esther, "for such a time as this" (Esther 4:14).

Peter's introduction is full of rich doctrine. Here in verse 1, he commences the book with a Trinitarian introduction. He tells us here that the source of our salvation is the Triune God. We are chosen by God the Father. We are sanctified by the Spirit. We are cleansed and called to obedience by the Son. Theologians often state it this way when they describe how each person of the Trinity works in our salvation; "The Father initiates our salvation, the Son accomplishes our salvation, and the Spirit applies our salvation." We could spend weeks mining the depths of this single verse and not exhaust the greatness of His love and grace toward us.

We are God's chosen people, and now Peter will explain to us how and for what purpose we have been called. The verse is lavished with prepositions modifying our position in God as the elect and chosen people of God. We are the elect and chosen people of God according to the foreknowledge of God. This word "foreknowledge" is the Greek *eklektos*. It is used of God's people in Romans 8:29, Romans 11:2, and 1 Peter 2:9, but it is also used of Jesus Himself here in 1 Peter 1:2. It illuminates for us the beautiful truth that God has not only chosen His people for redemption before the foundation of the world, but He has chosen Jesus as their Savior and the source of their redemption. God the Father has initiated our salvation, and He has given us a Savior. The work of the Spirit in our salvation is seen in the sanctifying work of the Spirit. This is both at the time of salvation by drawing our hearts, convicting us of sin, and then it is also a process of sanctification in which the Spirit conforms us to the image of Jesus. We are chosen and elect of God the Father, to be sanctified by the Spirit, to obey Jesus. At the cross, Jesus accomplished our salvation.

The picture here in 1 Peter is that we have been sprinkled with the blood of Christ. This is a reference back to Exodus 24 when the people of Israel entered a covenant with God, and Moses sprinkled the people in blood. The people responded to God with a promise that they would keep God's law, but they would never be able to keep the law in their own selves, and the old covenant of the law would point them to their need for a Savior and a new covenant. This new covenant came through Jesus (Matthew 26:26-29). The new covenant would do what the old covenant could never do—it would transform the hearts of God's people. This covenant would not be written on tablets of stone but on the hearts of God's chosen people (Jeremiah 31:31-33). While the old covenant would seek to regulate what we did, the new covenant in the person of Jesus changes who we are. We are His people called to be exiles in a world that is not our home. We find grace in the wilderness of this world because Jesus is with us every step of the way.

Peter ends his greeting with a blessing and a prayer that grace and peace would be multiplied and abundant in the life of the readers. This grace and peace are possible only because of the work of the Triune God in the heart and life of the believer. The believer can be covered in God's grace and filled with peace in the midst of suffering because of the glorious work of God in them.

―――――

We are God's chosen people.

In what ways do we as Christians live as chosen exiles in the world today?

How does it bring you comfort that God has not only chosen you as His child but chosen you for the life that He has given you?

How does this encourage you not to compare your life to others?

Read Exodus 24 to better understand the picture of us being sprinkled with the blood of Jesus. Then read Jeremiah 31:31–33 about the new covenant that came through Jesus. In what ways is the new covenant better than the old?

A LIVING HOPE

—

WEEK 1 | DAY 3

Read
1 PETER 1:3-5

Blessed. That is how this next passage of Scripture begins. It is a proclamation of the character of God. This blessing was customary in the Old Testament and at the beginning of worship in Hebrew culture. A blessing would be given in anticipation of the Messiah who was to come. But this blessing from Peter was different. Peter is praising and thanking God that the Messiah has come. He is praising God for keeping His promises just like He always does.

We are pointed here to the Father who is the initiator and cause of our salvation. And we are pointed to the Son through whom that salvation is made possible. This passage is overflowing with covenant language pointing us to the truth that God does what He has promised. Verse 3 tells us that salvation is made possible according to or because of the great mercy of God. The Greek here for "mercy" is *eleos,* and it is related to the Hebrew word *hesed* that speaks of God's covenant, faithful, steadfast love. It is this great steadfast and covenantal love and mercy by which God has caused us to be saved through the work of Jesus. Our salvation is a result of the initiating love of God. It is fully dependent on His grace and cannot be accomplished in any way by our own good works (Ephesians 2:8-9).

Peter tells us here that God has caused us to be born again, or made new, to a living hope through the power of the resurrection. Sometimes we think about hope as wishful thinking. The concept in our mind can almost make hope seem naive, but that is not the kind of hope that Peter is speaking about. We are called to a hope that is a confident expectation in what we know that God will do. We know that God will be faithful to His Word because we are confident in God Himself. It is interesting to think about how this hope had transformed Peter's own life. Peter had pushed against the idea of Jesus going to the cross (Matthew 16:22-23). Then Peter denied even knowing Jesus as He prepared to go to the cross (Matthew 26:69-75). Hope seemed lost as Jesus died on the cross bearing the weight of our sin and the weight of Peter's as well. But then three days later everything changed. Jesus rose from the dead, and hope resurrected as well. Hope did not die at the cross—it was the cross that brought forth an unshakable hope. After the resurrection, Peter was a changed man. He went on to preach of this powerful and unwavering hope because he himself had experienced it. Our hope is alive because Jesus is alive. And because Jesus is alive, we are alive. We have union with Him and new life in Him. We live with Him in expectant hope.

We have not only been given a living hope, but we have been secured an inheritance that is imperishable, undefiled, and unfading, and that is kept secure for us. The inheritance language reminds us of the importance of the Old Testament inheritance to the people of Israel. Inheritance language is found throughout the Old Testament. It was the expectant hope of the inheritance of the promised land that gave Israel hope as they wandered in the wilderness. And here Peter is telling us that our inheritance is better than the promise of land. The inheritance of land could be destroyed by the elements or destroyed by enemies, but our inheritance can never be destroyed. The inheritance of land could be contaminated by sin, but nothing can defile the inheritance that has been promised to us. The inheritance of land could fade like the grass (1 Peter 1:24), but our inheritance will never fade. And this inheritance of ours is kept or guarded by God. This inheritance is the fullness of our salvation. In this world we see just a glimpse of what God has prepared for His people, and we have the down-payment of the Holy Spirit in us (Ephesians 1:14), but someday we will see all that God has for His children.

We live in hope in the present because Jesus has in the past secured a future hope for us. The reality of our salvation is past, present, and future. The rich theology of 1 Peter is also the practicality and application that we need for our daily lives. Lest we think that this hope and inheritance are all about the future, Peter speaks right into our present situation as we live as strangers and exiles in this world. He tells us that while God is keeping and guarding an inheritance for us, He is also guarding and keeping us in this life through faith. This faith is not about our own accomplishment, but it is a gift of His grace. This faith is measured not by our feeble attempts to trust Him but by the trustworthiness of the One that we place our faith in. We can trust God in the waiting because God is with us in the waiting.

What do these verses tell us about our salvation and how God accomplishes it?

We have defined biblical hope as "confident expectation." How can you live a life that overflows with that kind of hope?

Look up and define "imperishable," "undefiled," "unfading," and "kept."
What does this tell us about our inheritance?

How does God's presence with you in this life as an exile in the world encourage you to press on?

Joy

WEEK 1 | DAY 4

Peter turns his thoughts toward the present reality of believers. He reveals for us that though part of our present situation as exiles in this world is to face a multitude of trials, our present reality is also one of rejoicing right in the midst of the trials that may come. We are not a hopeless people. Just yesterday we were reminded of our living hope found in Jesus, and today we are being reminded to live in hope in a world that is not our home. In 2 Corinthians 4:8-9 the apostle Paul spoke of believers as afflicted but not crushed, perplexed but not in despair, persecuted but not abandoned, struck down but not destroyed, and Jesus in the Sermon on the Mount spoke of the blessedness that comes from being persecuted for the sake of Christ (Matthew 5:10-12). This is the paradox of our faith and the gloriousness of the upside-down kingdom. There is blessing for following Jesus, even when the immediate result may be suffering. Jesus is our living hope, and because of Him, we can live in hope.

Rejoicing during suffering is counter-cultural. It doesn't make sense to the world around us. Verse 6 tells us that we rejoice in "this," but the interesting thing about this word in Greek is that it can just as easily be translated as "whom." Theologians are split on which it should be, but both are true. We rejoice in the "this" of all of what we have learned in verses 3-5, and we rejoice in the "whom" that they speak of. We rejoice in Jesus, and we rejoice in His work of salvation for us. Jesus is the source of our rejoicing, and He is the reason that we can face trials with joy. We can rejoice in our suffering because Jesus is with us in our suffering.

How comforting that Peter reminds us that our suffering is for a little while. It will not last forever. Just as this world is not our forever home, the trials that we face are not forever either. The trials of this world test or prove our faith (Job 23:10, Psalm 66:10, Proverbs 17:3, James 1:2-4). As gold is refined by fire, we are refined by our temporary trials. And our faith in those trials results in praise, glory, and honor for our Savior. Our trials today result in a someday glory. Peter is trying to fix our eyes on Jesus and fix our eyes on eternity. He wants us to focus on what is eternal and not be distracted by the temporary (Colossians 3:2). He is not minimizing our suffering; He is pointing us to the One who is with us in suffering and the hope that is to come. The glory to come is far greater than the grief of this world (2 Corinthians 4:17, Romans 4:18). We live in hope and look forward to the day when our hope will be fulfilled completely.

We are given a deeper picture of our faith as we are reminded that we love Jesus though we have not seen Him, and we believe even though we cannot see. Peter had seen Jesus. He had seen Him work miracles. He had watched Him die on the cross, and he had seen His risen body. Peter knew that the believers who read this letter had not, so he encourages them to trust even when they cannot see. In John 20:29, Jesus even spoke of the blessedness of believing even when you cannot see. It seems so fitting that Peter would give us this picture of faith in the middle of a section on suffering and trials. Isn't this what we must do each day as we face seasons of waiting, trials, and suffering? We must choose to trust that He is working, even though we cannot see what He is doing. We choose to believe the words of Romans 8:28, that God will work all things for the good of those that love Him. We choose to believe, even when we cannot see. We do not see Him with our eyes, but there is coming a day that we will. And for now, we can see His sovereign hand with the eyes of faith working every circumstance for our good.

And then right there in the midst of our sufferings and trials we rejoice. How interesting that Peter speaks of this joy in the present tense. Peter could have said that we will rejoice. He could have told us that someday when all of these trials are over we will be able to rejoice and know that it was all worth it. And while those things are true, that is not what Peter chooses to tell us here. Instead, he speaks in the present tense and tells us that as we believe we rejoice with joy. Right now. Right in the middle of the trials. We rejoice with joy that is inexpressible and glorious because of who He is. We can rejoice today because of what God has done already and because of what we know He will do.

We can live in joy and faith because He is our living hope. We can rejoice even in our suffering because He is working even when we cannot see. We can find peace in His presence no matter what troubles may come. How do we have joy in every situation? The answer may seem like the simple Sunday school answer, but it is true. We have joy because of Jesus.

———

Jesus is the source of our rejoicing,

and He is the reason that we can face trials with joy. We can rejoice in our suffering because Jesus is with us in our suffering.

What trials or situations in your life right now do you need to trust God in?

Read Job 23:10, Psalm 66:10, Proverbs 17:3, and James 1:2-4.
What insight do these verses give you about how our faith is refined like gold?

Has there ever been a time in your life when God worked in ways that you could not see at first? How does that encourage you to trust God today?

Look up the word "inexpressible," and write the definition below.
What does this tell you about the kind of joy that we have because of Jesus?

GLORY REVEALED

—

WEEK 1 | DAY 5

Peter has described for us who we are, and he has told us about our hope and purpose. He is about to shift his focus to how we are to live in this world, but before he does he points us to the Word. He points us to the Word that points us to the Word that became flesh (John 1:1).

Every part of Scripture points us to Jesus, and that is what Peter is going to remind us in these verses. This message of salvation that has been given to us was first given to the prophets of the Old Testament. Sometimes we are tempted to avoid the Old Testament. But we are urged here to recognize that Jesus is on every page. The Bible is the story of redemption. It is the story of God seeking to dwell with His people and seeking to rescue and restore. From the first promise of the gospel in Genesis 3:15 and the message that a Messiah would come to restore all that had been broken by sin, the Bible has been proclaiming Jesus with every breath. The prophets spoke of redemption and salvation. They predicted not only the glory of Christ but also His suffering. Jesus spoke of His impending suffering to Peter in Matthew 16:13-22. Peter had just declared that Jesus was the Messiah, but when Jesus said that He would have to suffer and die, Peter pushed back. He didn't even want to think about the possibility of Jesus suffering. But the glory always comes after the suffering. We, just like Peter, so often want the glory without the suffering. But we are called to live like Jesus, and this means that we will face trials and suffering in this life, but the glory of eternity is assured. Peter had learned these hard truths from experience. He had looked on while Jesus suffered, and now he himself had faced persecution, but he knew that the glory of Jesus in eternity was coming. Later in 1 Peter we will be encouraged that though we share in Christ's sufferings, His glory will one day be revealed. We like short cuts. But Jesus is our example, and the cross is our example of how glory comes through suffering. There would be no hope of redemption without the agony of the cross. God uses suffering. Suffering is never wasted when placed in the hands of our sovereign God.

The prophets were preaching the gospel of Jesus. They were declaring His coming suffering and coming glory. The prophets themselves did not fully understand the message that they were speaking, but they recorded the very words of God, not just for the benefit of themselves or those who lived during their ministry but for us! The prophets proclaimed the message of Jesus so that we could look at His Word and see Him on every page. These verses tell us how we should interpret all of Scripture. We should look for Jesus. We should look for the gospel. He is there! For the prophets of the Old Testament and even for the angels of heaven, the words

of Scripture seemed veiled and mysterious, but the coming of Jesus has revealed to us what the Old Testament spoke of. Jesus has been revealed for us.

Have you ever wondered what it would have been like to live in the times of Scripture and to see some of those events for yourself? If I had to choose a moment to be present I think I would go back to the events of Luke 24:13-35. In this passage after the resurrection, Jesus appears to a few followers though they don't know that it is Him, and He explains to them how all the prophets had pointed to Him. The disciples said that their hearts burned within them as He explained God's plan for all the ages to them. Can you imagine what it would have been like to hear Jesus tell how He was the fulfillment of every promise and covenant. Though it would be amazing to have been there that day, Peter is telling us that we have the ability to open God's Word ourselves with the power of the Spirit inside of us and see all that the prophets had spoken and how every word points to Jesus. This should stir our hearts to desire God's Word. This should make us long to read every word on every page. The prophets had a special role, but they could not fully understand all that their words meant. Even the angels desire to know the mysteries of salvation. We have received the gift of God's grace, and we have the gift of His Word before us that we can open and search for Him in. The Old and New Testaments are not two different messages. They are one message pointing to One Messiah. They are one message of grace. One story of redemption. May our hearts yearn for His Word as we seek to know Him more.

Read Matthew 16:13–22, and consider Peter's perspective before the cross and the resurrection. In light of what you have read so far in 1 Peter, how has Peter's perspective been changed by the cross and the empty tomb?

Why do you think it is that we want to rush to the message of glory without the message of suffering? How does a reminder that Jesus is our example of suffering give us comfort as we face our own suffering?

How do these verses impact the way that you read and study Scripture?

BLESSED BE THE
GOD AND FATHER
OF OUR LORD JESUS
CHRIST. *BECAUSE OF
HIS GREAT MERCY* HE
HAS GIVEN US *NEW
BIRTH INTO A LIVING
HOPE* THROUGH THE
RESURRECTION OF
JESUS CHRIST FROM
THE DEAD

—

1 PETER 1:3

WEEK 1

—

MEMORY
VERSE

WEEK ONE *reflection*

— 1 Peter 1:1-12 —

Paraphrase the passage from this week.

What did you observe from this week's text about God and His character?

What does the passage teach about the condition of mankind and about yourself?

How does this passage point to the gospel?

How should you respond to this passage? What is the personal application?

What specific action steps can you take this week to apply the passage?

Hope in Grace

WEEK 2 / DAY 1

Read
1 PETER 1:13

What we are commanded to do always flows from what God has already done for us. So this section begins with the word "therefore," and it tells us how to live in light of what God has already done for us. Peter began this letter with a glorious doxology praising God for our salvation, and now he is going to tell us how to live in light of the salvation that we have been given. The indicative comes before the imperatives. We are told what God has done, but now we are going to be urged to action.

The central command here is to set our hope on grace. Peter tells us what to do, but he also tells us how to do it. So we are commanded to set our hope completely on the grace that will be brought to us at the revelation of Jesus Christ. This is the same hope that we saw in verse 3. In verse 3 we saw that we have been born again to a living hope, and now we are being commanded to intentionally set our hope in the grace of Jesus. We see here the already but not yet of our faith. We have this same grace now because of the life, death, and resurrection of Jesus. But our hope will be fully realized someday when Jesus returns and all is restored. So we look forward not just with wishful thinking but with confident expectation that Jesus will bring to completion what He has begun (Philippians 1:6). We can live in this living hope. It isn't just a future hope — it is a hope that we experience right now and await its full consummation that will come with the return of Christ. Peter is urging us to place our hope in the gospel alone. The gospel is Jesus Himself. Grace is Jesus Himself.

So how do we do it? What does this mean for life? Peter tells us exactly how we are supposed to do this. The first thing we are told to do is to prepare our minds for action. The word usually translated as "preparing" or "ready" literally means "to gird up your loins." This first century imagery is foreign to us, but it would have brought a vivid picture to the minds of the original readers. During this time the men wore long robe-like garments. But if they needed to be ready for battle they would gird up their loins, or wrap their robe in a special way, so that they could move quickly and unhindered. They had to get rid of all their obstacles. In the same way, we must prepare our minds for battle. We must get rid of all of the things that distract us and hold us back from following Jesus. It is interesting to note that it is our minds that are spoken of here. This is more than just our intellect, but it is our whole person. Our minds impact every part of us. That is why Paul in Romans 12:2 commanded us to be transformed by the renewing of our minds. We must know the truth of God's Word if we are going to act on it, and transformation starts in our minds.

Jesus spoke of the same truth when he told his disciples in Luke 12:35 to stay dressed for action or be ready for service. And undoubtedly, Peter would have also been thinking of a very key passage in the Old Testament and the history of Israel. On the night of the first Passover, God commanded the children of Israel to eat that first Passover meal ready to go, with their sandals on their feet, and their staff in their hands (Exodus 12:11). We are being commanded to do the same thing here. We must be ready and prepared to face this life. Setting our hope on Jesus does not mean that we sit back and do nothing, it means that we are ready to march into battle in His strength.

The other thing that we must do as we set our hope on Jesus is to be sober-minded. We are to be sober and not drunk. To be drunk is to be controlled by something outside of you. But this is not just speaking of literal drunkenness. Alcohol is not the only thing that can intoxicate us. We can be drunk with pride, anger, bitterness, greed, worry, etc., but Peter is telling us that the only thing that should control us is the Spirit within us (Ephesians 5:18). We must not be controlled by anything but Jesus.

In order to set our hope on Jesus, we are going to need to get rid of the things that hold us back, and we are going to need to lay aside the things that intoxicate us. We are going to have to fix our eyes firmly on Jesus and place our hope fully and completely in Him.

Go back and read 1 Peter 1:1–12, and make note of all the things that God has done.

Now look closely at 1 Peter 1:13, and think about what the relationship is between what God has done in verses 1–12 and what we are commanded to do in verse 13. Record your thoughts below.

What are the things that distract you from setting your hope fully or completely on Jesus?

What would it look like to set your hope fully or completely on Jesus?

BE HOLY BECAUSE HE IS HOLY

—

WEEK 2 / DAY 2

34

Read
1 PETER 1:14-21

Having set our hope completely on the grace of Christ, Peter now instructs us on how to live. We are commanded to be obedient children. We are to follow the Word of God and not the desires and thoughts that we once did. We are not what we once were. Ephesians 2:1-5 tells us that we were once dead in our sins, but God has made all the difference for us, and through His grace He has made us new and united us with Christ. So when Peter then commands us to be holy because our God is holy, he is not talking about us trying hard in our own strength to be good people. The idea of even a believer earning God's favor by good works is anti-gospel. We are not called to be holy in our own strength but in His strength. Because we have been made new and united with Christ, we can walk in the holiness that He has called us to. Doing flows from being. We can live holy lives only because we have been transformed and made new. Sanctification is the process of being made holy. We are called to holiness and sanctification. We are called to abide and allow the Spirit to transform us. We are commanded to be holy as He is holy. And we cannot become like Him if we do not know who He is. In order for us to become like Him, we must behold the glory of God. We learn holiness by learning who He is, because He is holy.

Peter will again speak of the beauty of the gospel. He takes us back to the gospel and reminds us that holiness is only possible because of salvation. We have been ransomed from our sin and from the past that enslaved us. We have been bought and redeemed with the most precious thing, the blood of Christ. Redemption is not free. Though it costs us nothing, it cost Jesus everything. We pursue holiness as a response to the great grace that we have been given. This precious blood is like a lamb without blemish. Peter here uses the language and imagery of the Passover (Exodus 12), and the same imagery that John the Baptist used in John 1:29 when he said, "Behold the Lamb of God." We are pointed in this passage to Jesus who is the source of our salvation.

Then Peter makes a stunning statement. Back in 1 Peter 1:2, Peter had said that we as believers were foreknown by God. Now here in 1 Peter 1:20, he tells us that Jesus was also foreknown before the foundation of the world. Our redemption and our Redeemer were God's plan from the foundation of the world. Jesus is not Plan B or an afterthought. These words echo the words of Peter's sermon in Acts 2:23-24 where we learned that Jesus' death was the definite plan from the beginning. The plan of salvation has been slowly revealed through the Scriptures. The Old Testament believers had glimpses of what God was doing through covenants and the promise of the Messiah,

but it is not until Jesus came that the plan was revealed fully. From the foundation of the world to the last times, the plan has always been Jesus. Beginning to end—the focus is Jesus.

He has come, and He has died just as was promised—for the sake of His people. For you. This is what spurs us on to holiness. It is the never-ending, overflowing, overwhelming love of God. We do not seek to live holy lives because of any goodness in ourselves but because of Christ in us and because of our overwhelming gratitude for who He is and what He has done for us.

And the passage ends with another reminder of hope. Our faith and our hope are in God alone. We can live in this world as elect exiles because of Jesus. We can live in hope because of Jesus. We can face trials because of Jesus. We can pursue holiness because of Jesus.

Because we have been made new and united with Christ, we can walk in the holiness that He has called us to.

How do we grow in holiness through the strength of God?

How does the fact that God has foreknown both us as believers and our redemption through Jesus expand your understanding of salvation?

How should the understanding that Jesus has been the plan since the beginning change the way you read the Old Testament?

How does the truth of God's unshakable plan of all time encourage you to live in hope?

The Word of
The Lord
Endures Forever

WEEK 2 | DAY 3

Read
1 PETER 1:22-25

God's Word endures. This is the message that Peter is proclaiming to us as elect exiles. Our souls have been purified or cleansed by obedience to the truth. This is the Word of God, or more specifically it is the gospel (Ephesians 1:13). The cleansing and purification of our souls is not possible in our own strength. Transformation is only possible because of the gospel. Paul would say in his letter to the Romans that the gospel is the power of God for those who believe (Romans 1:16). The gospel is what makes us alive, and it is what transforms us.

But Peter also tells us one of the reasons for this purification, that we would love each other. We should love our brothers and sisters in Christ fervently and constantly from a pure heart. Purity of heart is a mark of a believer and one of the things that Jesus names in the Sermon on the Mount (Matthew 5:8). The gospel calls us to purity of heart, and it calls us to community. Being born into the family of God means being born into a new family. We are born into God's church and into His chosen people. And while the saying is true that where there are people there are problems, it is also true that were there are people there can be partnership. We are made partners in the work of the gospel through the work of the gospel in us.

And all of this is possible because we have been born again. We have experienced regeneration and have been given new life in Christ. Peter points out that this life is not of the perishable seed of this earth, because everything on this earth dies. Instead this is life that is born out of the living, imperishable, abiding, and enduring Word of God. The gospel gives life. The Word of God gives life. Not just temporary and transient life but steadfast and enduring life.

And then Peter does something amazing. He quotes from the book of Isaiah. Now Peter quotes from the Old Testament many times in this short letter, but this quote is particularly significant to us. He quotes from Isaiah 40 to remind us that human life is like the grass that perishes, but God's Word endures forever. But for his listeners who knew the Old Testament and for Peter himself, the significance of Isaiah 40 was nearly unparalleled. The book of Isaiah contains 66 chapters, and because of this it has been likened to being the Bible in miniature form. The book is divided into two books much like the testaments in our Bible. The first section of Isaiah has 39 chapters, just like the 39 books of the Old Testament. And the second section begins with Isaiah 40 and is called The Book of Consolation. It is this pivotal chapter that Peter quotes from. So though the words that Peter quotes illustrate the truth he is trying to drive home, he

also knew that the words would bring with it a flood of memories of this important chapter. Much like this letter that Peter is writing, the fortieth chapter of Isaiah is written to exiles that needed to be reminded of hope. They needed to be reminded to wait and hope on the Lord who would be the comfort of His people in the time of exile. It is the same message that Peter is proclaiming here to the new people of God. God is our hope during our exile in this world.

After quoting from Isaiah 40, Peter says that this message from Isaiah is the gospel that was proclaimed to his readers. The message from Isaiah is the message of the gospel. It is the message of hope in the Messiah. For the Jews that Isaiah proclaimed the message to, they looked forward to a coming Messiah. For us today, we look back on a Messiah who has come and brought comfort and hope to His people. And yet at the very same time we look ahead to the day when our risen Savior will return and bring final comfort to us. God's living and abiding Word is a message of hope for His people. We are a people of hope because of Jesus. So Peter's message in this first chapter is to live in hope. To live life through the lens of the gospel. To be assured that this life and the struggles that we face here are temporary, but God's Word endures forever. The hope of the gospel is greater than the pain of this world. We have gospel-hope because we have Jesus.

———

Transformation is only possible because of the gospel.

How does God's Word/the gospel purify and cleanse our souls?

In our culture, love and truth are often thought of as being opposites, but in these verses, we see that our obedience to the truth leads to love. Why do you think that this is true?

Read Isaiah 40. How do the words of Isaiah bring comfort to us today? How does this chapter point us toward the gospel?

What does it mean to look at our life through the lens of the gospel?

DESIRE THE WORD

—

WEEK 2 | DAY 4

Read
1 PETER 2:1-3

In light of what we have just seen at the end of chapter 1 about the Word of God and the power of the gospel, we come to the beginning of chapter 2. It begins with a word that points us back to what we have just learned to show us that these concepts are deeply connected. We are then shown what we should not be and what we should be. We see several things that we should put off or get rid of in our lives. Peter has just told us about the power of the gospel to transform us, and now he tells us to not go back to the things that the gospel has rescued us from. The traits listed here stand in contrast to the fruit of the Spirit that grows in the life of a believer (Galatians 5:22-23). Throughout Scripture we see numerous commands for us to put off the old man and the works of the flesh (Romans 13:12, Ephesians 4:22 and 25, Colossians 3:8, James 1:21). But we also see positive commands to put on the new man and the fruit and works of the Spirit, and even to put on Christ (Ephesians 4:24, Romans 13:14, Colossians 3:6-17). It is clear that following Jesus is both an instant salvation and a process of growing in sanctification or as Peter says here, growing up into salvation.

So how does that happen? We must desire or long for the milk of the Word. Our deeds will not change if our desires do not change. We must desire the Word of God and feast on its life-giving sustenance in order for us to be sustained and to grow. Peter has already spoken of salvation as a new birth, and now he continues that illustration by telling us that we should desire God's Word like a newborn desires milk. Newborns are obsessed with food and consumed by their need for it, and we should be the same way in our relation to the Word of God. We should be obsessed with the Word of God. We should be consumed by our need for the life-giving Word. Milk is necessary for an infant. In the same way, the spiritual milk of the Word of God is necessary and vital for us as believers. Without the Word of God in our lives on a daily basis we risk being diagnosed with a spiritual case of "failure to thrive." Just as a newborn must have proper nourishment to grow, we must be nourished by the Word of God to grow in Christ.

In verse 1 we see the problem of the things that should not be in our lives, and in verse 2 we see the solution to the problem. The Word of God is the cure for our sin-sick hearts. As we view our life through the lens of the gospel and see the way that God sees, we begin to hate our sin, even the sins, like those mentioned in verse 1, that are viewed as more acceptable sins. When we remember the price that Christ paid for our sin, we desire to put it to death as Paul commanded in Colossians 3:5. And then we desire the Word of God and the Spirit of God to transform us

into the image of Christ. This is the process of sanctification and the present and future aspect of our salvation. Though we are presently saved as believers in Christ, we are also awaiting a day when we will be freed not just from the penalty of sin (justification) and the power of sin (sanctification) but also from sin's presence (glorification). There is a future aspect to our present-day salvation. It is another part of the already but not yet of the Christian life. We possess something that we also long for. We are justified, and we are being sanctified through the Word of God, and we will be glorified someday. In Romans, Paul speaks of this glorification in the past tense though it is yet future for us. It is a reminder to us that what God has promised is as good as done. He will do what He has said He will do. He will be faithful.

Peter ends this passage by quoting Psalm 34:8. The reason that we long for the Word of God, and the reason that we can be changed, is because we have tasted the goodness of the Lord. We have experienced who He is. We have experienced the power of the gospel of Christ to change us from who we once were to who He is calling us to be. As we open His Word each day, we are declaring with our life that we need Him. We have tasted His goodness, and we long to taste it anew each and every day.

Using a dictionary or concordance/lexicon, look up the things that we are commanded to put off or get rid of. Write the definitions below.

What are the opposites of those things? Reference the things that we are commanded to put on in Colossians 3:9–17, as well as the fruit of the Spirit in Galatians 5:22–23 to help you understand what we should put on.

How does spiritual growth come through the Word of God? Look up Hebrews 4:12, 2 Timothy 3:16, and Isaiah 55:10–11 to better understand how the Word works in us.

In what ways have you tasted the goodness of God?

Living Stones

WEEK 2 | DAY 5

Read
1 PETER 2:4-8

In chapter one of 1 Peter we were shown the picture of salvation and urged to trust in a living hope and the living Word. As we move further into the second chapter, Peter is helping us to better understand our identity and our union with Christ. Remember, 1 Peter is written to the elect exiles, and as believers in the church today we can closely identify with them. But Peter is reminding us that our identity is not found in being an exile; our identity is tied to who Jesus is because we are united to Him. Our identity is based on whose we are, not who we are.

So, before Peter tells us who we are, he tells us who Jesus is. He describes Christ as a living stone that is chosen and honored by God, though He is rejected by men. It is interesting that Peter would use this description of Jesus since Jesus had once called Peter a rock as well (Matthew 16:13-20). Though Peter's name was originally Simon, Jesus gave him the name Peter which means "rock." Yet here Peter does not reference himself as the rock. This is a reminder to us that we cannot be what God has called us to be apart from Christ. Peter would fumble and make many mistakes, but his position and identity was firm and secure in Jesus.

Jesus is described as the rock, and this is drawing on several Old Testament passages that spoke of this rock and cornerstone. In its immediate context it was full of temple imagery, but Jewish tradition also identified this rock to be the coming Messiah. Peter quotes three Old Testament passages to tell us that Jesus is that rock that was promised. He is the firm and secure cornerstone. He is the One who was rejected by men but chosen and honored by God. He would be the stone of stumbling to all those that would reject Him in unbelief. But He would also be the cornerstone of His people.

Jesus was the chosen and precious cornerstone, and yet when He came to this world, He was rejected. He was rejected by the religious leaders and rulers that crucified Him, He was rejected by the nation of Israel, and He is rejected by all that refuse to believe the truth of the gospel (Matthew 21:33-46, Romans 9:30-33, 1 Peter 2:7-8). Yet even the unbelief of many was foreknown by God (Psalm 118:22-23, Isaiah 8:14-15). Jesus would be rejected, and Jesus would suffer, yet even this was part of God's sovereign plan, and this is good news for believers in exile that face rejection and suffering. God is sovereign over every moment of suffering, and He will bring good from it. Though we share in His suffering, there will be a day when we rejoice in His glory (1 Peter 4:13).

Though He was rejected by men, He was chosen by God. Peter will then use the same language to speak of us as believers. In chapter one Peter told us how Jesus was foreknown (1 Peter 1:20), and how we were foreknown (1 Peter 1:2). Now he tells us that Jesus is chosen and is a living stone, and then he tells us that we are chosen as living stones as well. We have a living hope, and we are living stones just as Jesus is a living stone and is our living hope. Jesus is a living stone, and we are living stones as well. We are being built up into a spiritual house. Very similar language is used by Paul in Ephesians 2:20-22 where we see that the temple of God that is the church is built up as we are built up in Him. We have union with Christ, and we are being built up in Him. The spiritual house of God is grown as believers are added to the church and as the people of God grow in sanctification. The living stones and household of God that is described here is plural. It is speaking of the church as God's chosen people. Christians are made for community. We were never meant to live this life on our own but in the fellowship of the family of God. We may be exiles in the world, but we belong in the church.

The temple language here is a consistent theme in Scripture. Throughout the narrative of God's Word, we see the dwelling place of God. In Genesis we saw how Adam and Eve dwelt with God in Eden (Genesis 1-2). Then we saw God dwell with His people through the tabernacle (Exodus 25:8) and then the temple (2 Chronicles 6:2). When Jesus came to earth we are told that He came and dwelt (literally tabernacled) among us (John 1:14), and in the New Testament we learn that God dwells in His people who are the temple of God (Ephesians 2:20-22, 1 Corinthians 6:19, 1 Peter 2:4-6). In the book of Revelation, we learn that there will come a day when there will be no temple because God will dwell in the midst of His people (Revelation 21:3, 22-23). We are God's people and He dwells with us and in us. Our God is Emmanuel. So, as we walk through this life we can be confident that though we may face suffering, we will never do it alone (Matthew 28:19-20). We live this life in union with Christ who is our solid foundation and cornerstone.

———

We have a living hope and we are living stones
just as Jesus is a living stone and is our living hope.

How does it bring us comfort as exiles to know that Jesus was an exile in this world as well?

Peter would have heard Jesus quote one of these Old Testament passages in the book of Matthew. Read Matthew 21:33–46 and think about how this would have deepened what Peter meant when he wrote these words, and how we can better understand it. Think about the implications of the prophets of the Old Testament as the servants and Jesus as the Son. What was Jesus trying to tell the religious leaders?

Verse 5 says that we are being built up in order to offer spiritual sacrifices. Read Romans 12:1–2 for insight into what our spiritual sacrifice is and record what you find below.

Read and paraphrase John 1:14.

BUT AS THE
ONE WHO CALLED
YOU IS *HOLY*,
YOU ALSO ARE TO
BE *HOLY* IN ALL
YOUR CONDUCT

—

1 PETER 1:15

WEEK 2

MEMORY
VERSE

WEEK TWO *reflection*

— 1 Peter 1:13 - 2:8 —

Paraphrase the passage from this week.

What did you observe from this week's text about God and His character?

What does the passage teach about the condition of mankind and about yourself?

How does this passage point to the gospel?

How should you respond to this passage? What is the personal application?

What specific action steps can you take this week to apply the passage?

HIS CHOSEN PEOPLE

—

WEEK 3 | DAY 1

We have union with Christ, and that makes all the difference. We come to these important verses, and we are reminded that all of these beautiful declarations are possible only because of our union with Christ. Peter has just referenced Old Testament prophecy in telling us that just as Jesus is a living stone, we too are living stones that are being built up into a spiritual household. Now Peter will reference several more Old Testament passages to give us an even deeper view of who we are and what Christ has done for us.

Peter is making a shocking statement as he speaks to Christians. He is saying that they are Israel. They are a spiritual Israel. The church is the chosen people of God that is united with Jesus. These two short verses reference three key passages that will help us better understand what Peter is saying. These passages are Exodus 19:5-6, Isaiah 43, and Hosea 2:23. Peter references these passages to show us how they have been fulfilled in Jesus and how we experience that fulfillment in Christ.

In Exodus 19, the people of Israel had been delivered from Egypt and were at the base of Mount Sinai. God was giving them the law and a covenant that if they would keep the law there would be blessing, but if they disobeyed the law, there would be great consequence. In verses 5 and 6, God tells them that if they will obey the covenant they will be His treasured possession, a kingdom of priests, and a holy nation. There on Mount Sinai the people promised that they would do everything that the Lord had commanded. If you remember back to the Old Testament though, you know that they did not. They did not, and they could not. They could not keep the law in their own strength. But there was One that would keep the law. Jesus came as the promised Messiah. He lived the perfect life that we could not live, and He died the death that we deserved. On another mountain generations later, Jesus spoke the words of the Sermon on the Mount and said that He had not come to abolish the law but to fulfill it (Matthew 5:17-18). His perfect life and His sacrificial death did just that. Jesus fulfilled what Israel never could. Now in Him, we take part in these promises made long ago. We are a treasured possession, a kingdom of priests, and a holy nation because we are in Him.

In Isaiah 43 we find the message of hope and deliverance to God's people in exile in Babylon. The people of God had broken the covenant and found themselves in exile experiencing judgment for their sin. But God would bring a message of hope through the prophet Isaiah. God would not leave his people in exile; He would make a way for them. The hope of Israel and of all the world is the Messiah who they longed for. Jesus is our hope. Isaiah 43:1 speaks of God's people as redeemed and called by name, and that redemption was made possible through the cross. Isaiah 43:20-21 speaks of this chosen people that God had created for Himself so that they could praise Him. Peter draws on this exile imagery when he addresses his letter to the elect exiles, and then he shows us that we as the people of God are now part of this chosen remnant called out of every tribe, tongue, and nation. We are the chosen people who have been called from darkness into light. Just as God spoke light into darkness in Genesis 1:1, He has spoken light into the darkness of our lives and called us into His light by His Word. Now our purpose is to declare His glory. We were made for worship.

In Hosea 2:23, we encounter the people of Israel again in their covenant unfaithfulness. Though God has pursued them, they have rejected Him. In their unfaithfulness, the people had been called "No Mercy," and "Not My People." But God in His steadfast love had promised a day when "No Mercy" would be shown mercy, and "Not my people" would be made a people of God. This is our story as believers. We were far from God but have been brought near by the blood of Christ (Ephesians 2:13). We were under the wrath of God, but mercy has been extended to us.

Union with Christ makes all the difference. Called from darkness to light. Made a new creation. Chosen in Him. Holy in Him. A royal priesthood hidden in the Great High Priest. A people in Him. So many things that this verse tells us that we are, but all of them are only made possible in Him. We have nothing to bring to the table, yet in Him we have been given everything. We are, because He is.

———

Now in Him, we take part in these promises made long ago.

We are a treasured possession, a kingdom of priests, and a holy nation because we are in Him.

Make a list of all the things these verses say that we are.

What do these verses say that our purpose is? Isaiah 43:20–21 also gives us the answer.

Look up the word "union," and write the definition below.

Read 1 Peter 2:1–10. Make a list of the ways that Jesus is described and the way that we are described. How does this chapter point to our hope in Him?

Strangers and Exiles

WEEK 3 / DAY 2

Have you ever felt out of place? Have you ever felt like you didn't belong? Peter reminds us here that we should feel that way about this world. We are here on a mission, but this is not our home. We are strangers in a foreign land. We are children far from home. We are ambassadors to a foreign nation on a kingdom mission.

Peter addresses his readers as beloved or dear friends. Though they were certainly beloved to Peter, they were also beloved of their Heavenly Father. The word "beloved" was used of Jesus on multiple occasions (Mark 1:11, 9:7, 2 Peter 1:17, Ephesians 1:6), and simply by using this word, Peter identifies us with Christ. Our status as beloved of the Father is tied to our union with Christ. We are beloved because we are in the Beloved. Peter echoes back to the opening of this letter. We are strangers and exiles. Peter takes great care to remind believers of our identity in Christ before speaking of our conduct. Our conduct should stem from our identity. We live for Christ because we are Christ's. We serve Him because we love Him. We worship Him because we have been redeemed. We live lives of grateful obedience because He has done everything for us.

The language of this command is urgent. We are to abstain from the sinful desires of our flesh. We are to declare war on the sin that wages war against us. This life is a battle. In Ephesians 6, the apostle Paul urged us to put on the armor of God and now Peter uses battle language to remind us that we must fight against sin. In Colossians 3:5, Paul tells us to put our sin to death. We are urged by Scripture to not mess around with sin. Sin is serious, and it is a slippery slope. Galatians 5:16-26 contrasts for us the works of the flesh and the fruit of the Spirit. The passage lists out a variety of kinds of sin. Some are outward and visible while others are inward heart attitudes. And both kinds need to be eradicated from the life of the believer. Our desires have been changed. We have been given new life. Now we must flee from what we once were and allow the Holy Spirit to transform us through His power.

As we fight sin and live honorable lives before the world, the world will start to take notice. The gospel transforms culture. It is not us as believers but the power that is in us. The gospel should be evidenced by our actions. And the purpose of our honorable lives is to bring glory to God alone.

Peter is going to share several areas of life that we should demonstrate submission through. The first one that he names here in verse 13 is that we should submit to the civil authorities.

We should be respectful citizens in this land that is not our home. The people that Peter was writing to were living under civil authorities who were not believers and that fought against Christians. Yet Peter tells these Christians that they should honor those who have been placed over them. Our place in civil life is not to slander our leaders on social media but to pray for them on our knees. We are commanded to show honor to everyone, even those who we disagree with. There may come a time when we have to stand against authorities if they would try to force us to do evil or keep us from doing what is right, but as much as we can we are commanded to live honorable lives showing honor to all people. As we live as servants of Christ in a world that is foreign to us, we silence our enemies and point the world to the beauty of the gospel. We are out of place here, but we have a job to do. Our everyday lives serve to bring glory to Christ.

———

This life is a battle.

We are to declare war on the sin that wages war against us.

How should our identity as Christians shape our actions?

Read Galatians 5:16–26. Make a list of the desires of the flesh and a list of the fruit of the Spirit.

Colossians 3:5 tells us to put our sin to death. What sin do you need to put to death? What fruit of the Spirit needs to be cultivated in your life right now?

In what practical ways can you honor civil authorities? Why do you think that this is often difficult?

FOLLOW HIM

—

WEEK 3 | DAY 3

Peter continues to talk about submission and now addresses servants. The group of people being addressed here are those who are household slaves or servants. This form of slavery was much different than the racial and horrific slavery of America's past. It was much different, and yet there was still a prevalence of masters who abused their role of authority. Some were cruel and unjust. Paul had encouraged servants to pursue freedom if given the opportunity but also to not allow their position in life to hinder them from serving the Lord recognizing that they are living for God and not man (1 Corinthians 7:21-24). Because of who Jesus is, we can face anything in this world, and that is the message that Peter is speaking to these believers.

We likely have never felt the injustice of slavery or servitude. Yet most of us have experienced injustice of some kind. We have been treated unfairly or been asked to submit to a rule or leader that we did not agree with. These words of Peter's are just as valuable and timely for us as they were for those who lived in the direct context that he spoke of. With our modern outlook on life it seems that our default reaction to something or someone that we do not agree with is to say that those we disagree with do not deserve our respect. But Jesus reminded us in Luke 6:32-36 that it is easy to love and show mercy to those you agree with, but as followers of Jesus we should extend love to the unlovable and even to those that would be cruel and unjust to us. Though we likely do not experience these situations in the context of slavery, we may experience injustice in the workplace, from government, from a customer service representative, a family member, or even in the church. Our lives have no shortage of moments and situations of injustice, but we are told here that we can endure these situations with dignity and respect and with our hearts conscious or mindful of God through it all. This is living in the upside-down kingdom where the first are last and the last are first.

Our humanity pushes against suffering of any kind. Peter was well aware of this tendency. In Matthew 16 right after Peter had declared that Jesus was the Messiah, Jesus began to tell His disciples about the suffering that He would endure. Peter protested at the thought of Jesus suffering. He didn't want it to be true. Jesus rebuked Peter and told him that he was seeing things only from man's perspective. And then Jesus went on to tell the disciples that if they wanted to follow Him, they would need to take up their cross and follow Him. It is important to note that this command to take up our cross happens before Jesus went to the cross. Perhaps it helps us to understand how the disciples seemed so confused by this upside-down kingdom language. The

message of the kingdom does not make sense to us apart from the Spirit within us. We must begin to see our lives from an eternal perspective and not merely an earthly one.

But then Peter makes an even more startling statement in verse 21. Peter speaks of suffering, and then he tells us that we were called to this. Called to suffer? How can that be? But Peter reminds us that we are called to suffer just as Christ was called to suffer. Jesus suffered for us, and in His suffering He left an example for us of what it means to follow Him. We are exiles here. And in this land that is not our final home we will face suffering. But we do not do it alone. Jesus has gone before us to be a perfect example for us. We can count it joy to follow Him and to suffer as He suffered. We rejoice as we share in the sufferings of the One who suffered for us (1 Peter 4:13). And that suffering is overflowing with living hope because we know that this world is not our home.

The road of following Jesus leads us to the cross. The path of discipleship is marked with suffering. And yet we can face that suffering with confidence because our suffering is not a divine oversight but a divine calling. We are called to follow—called to lay down our pride and take up the cross.

We know that this world is not our home.

Is there an area in your life in which you have experienced injustice? How can you react to that in a Christlike way?

Read Matthew 16:21–28. How does this passage help you to understand Peter who was writing this? What does it mean to take up our cross and follow Jesus?

In Romans 13:1–3 we are commanded to be subject to authorities. Yet in Acts 5:29 we are commanded to obey God rather than man. How do these verses go together and how do they impact the way that we understand this passage?

How does 1 Peter 2:21 and the truth that we have been called to suffer as Christ has change your perspective on your own trials?

The Path of the Cross

WEEK 3 / DAY 4

Read
1 PETER 2:21-25

We are called to walk the path of the cross. We are called to follow the example of our Savior. Peter reminds us that Christ has suffered for us. He is our atoning sacrifice. He suffered for us, but He also suffered for our example. We are called to follow in the steps of Jesus. We are called to suffer and called to serve and to trust God every step of the way. The path of the cross is marked by suffering, but it ends in victory. Victory is sure for the children of God.

The passage describes the suffering of the Savior. The words echo the words of Isaiah 53 and lift our gaze to the cross and the character of the Savior. Jesus lived the perfect life that we could not live, and then He died the death that we deserved. He did not sin, but He bore our sin. He did not utter one lie. He was accused and reviled, and He did not return the reviling and accusation. He suffered for our sake, and though He had all power, He did not threaten His persecutors. He suffered for us. He bore our sin upon that cruel and barbaric cross.

But as we come to these words and are reminded that we are called to follow Him in His suffering and called to endure for His sake, we must also remember that we were once the persecutors. We were once the enemies of God (Romans 5:10). We were the ones who nailed Him to the cross. It was our sin that caused Him to cling to the cross when ten thousand angels could have carried Him away. He stayed on the cross for us. He bore the weight of our sin and satisfied the wrath of God for us. The heaviness of the cross reminds us of the debt that we have been forgiven and the grace that He has shown us. And the mercy that He has extended to us enables us to show mercy to those who would accuse us or sin against us. We can face suffering with confidence because the cross has secured our victory.

Jesus endured suffering without sin. Instead of retaliating for the injustice that had come upon Him, He entrusted Himself to the Father. Peter reminds us of Christ's example and encourages us to do the same. We can face suffering, slander, and trials by placing our faith in the Lord who always does what is right and good. He will not allow us to face difficulty unless it is what is best for us. As we walk through suffering we can place not just our situation but ourselves in the loving hands of God.

Jesus went to the cross for us. His suffering is our healing. He has given us salvation so that we would die to sin and live to righteousness. Jesus died so that we could die to sin and so that we

could be alive to God (Romans 6:11). We must not take lightly the sin that Christ died for. Paul commands us to put our sin to death (Colossians 3:5). We have died to sin through salvation and now we must fight against the sin in our hearts.

Peter ends this chapter by reminding us of the truth that God is our Shepherd (Psalm 23, Ezekiel 34). The Shepherd of our souls will not leave us in our wandering. He will come after us and call us back to Himself. The Shepherd will leave the ninety-nine to come after the one (Matthew 18:10-14). The Shepherd will call His sheep by name (John 10:3). The Shepherd will call His sheep by name and be the Good Shepherd (John 10). Our loving Shepherd will care for our souls and will keep watch over our hearts. He will lead us through every trial and testing and will bring us safely to the other side.

Peter who had once pushed against suffering (Matthew 16:21-28) now declares for us that it is grace to walk the path that Jesus walked. As we encounter suffering and struggle in this life, our hearts are firmly fixed on the One who is greater than suffering and has suffered for us. Suffering fixes our gaze on Jesus.

We are called to follow in the steps of Jesus.

We are called to suffer and called to serve and to trust God every step of the way.

In what ways are we called to follow the example of Jesus? Is there a specific area of your life right now that you need to follow His example in?

Read Isaiah 53. Describe the character of Jesus as seen in this passage.

In what ways are we tempted to retaliate when others hurt us?
How can we respond as Jesus would?

How can you continually entrust yourself and your situation to the Lord?
How does entrusting ourselves to Him bring comfort in our circumstances?

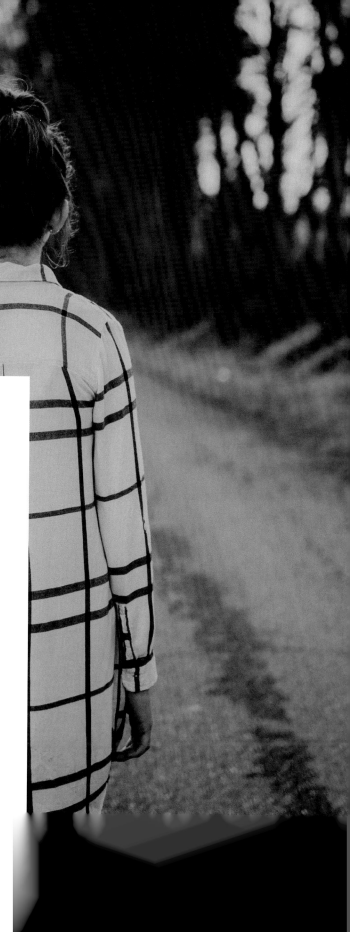

A LIFE THAT PROCLAIMS THE GOSPEL

—

WEEK 3 | DAY 5

Read

1 PETER 3:1-7

Ordinary obedience proclaims the gospel. This is the message that Peter proclaims. When we obey the Lord and follow Him, our lives proclaim to the world around us the truth of the gospel. As chapter three begins, Peter continues to speak to those living in this world as exiles, and he addresses wives of unbelieving husbands. He exhorts them to submit or be subject to their unbelieving husbands so that these men may be won to Christ. Peter knows that these wives with husbands who were not believers would desperately want their husbands to come to Christ, so he encourages them. Their unbelieving spouse may not want to hear the message of the gospel, but as the wife follows the Lord and lives a holy life, their husbands will be drawn to Christ.

Peter is not telling them not to speak the message of the gospel; he is telling them to also live it out. The temptation would be for these wives to nag their husbands and seek to manipulate their situations to coerce their husbands to faith, but Peter knows that is not what will soften the hard hearts of these men. Peter continues by telling the women to focus on their inward and not their outward beauty. Women for centuries have been tempted to gain the affection and approval of men through their beauty. Peter speaks to this by instructing women to not place their value in beauty or in things, but to find their worth in Christ alone. Instead of finding worth and investing only in the things that are temporary and fleeting—the believer is to cultivate inward beauty as we grow in sanctification.

The text speaks of the imperishable beauty of a gentle and quiet spirit. These words have been many times misunderstood. They do not prohibit women from having different personalities; instead the verse speaks of our spirit and our character. These words are not only feminine qualities, in fact Jesus describes Himself in nearly the same words in Matthew 11:29, and gentleness is listed in the fruit of the Spirit in Galatians 5:23. These qualities are not just for women; they are for all disciples of Jesus.

In the Greco-Roman culture that Peter wrote to, women would have been expected to submit to the religion of their husbands and not have friendships outside of his. So, a woman who had become a disciple and had a new community in the church was a social oddity. Despite the fact that a Christian woman married to an unbeliever would have been counter-cultural during this time, Peter encourages his readers that they can still live holy lives in front of their spouse. The example is given of Sarah and Abraham. Sarah is said to have spoken of Abraham as

lord, and this is simply a term of respect. Sarah did not slander her husband or talk behind his back disrespectfully. Sarah was not a weak woman — she was a strong woman. She regularly shared her opinions with Abraham, and he listened to her. She was far from a perfect woman, but she trusted God. We see her walking courageously into many situations including when her husband was called to go to a foreign land that God told him to go to (Genesis 12) and when Abraham would be told by God to sacrifice their only son (Genesis 22). We must be reminded that we are called to be Christ-like and to trust God above all. We are called to entrust ourselves and our situations to God alone as we learned in 1 Peter 2:23. He is trustworthy.

Peter then turns his attention to husbands and tells them to in the same way live with their wives in an understanding manner. They are commanded to show her honor. This passage leaves no space for abuse or the misuse of power. Women are designated as the weaker vessel, and this references the fact that typically women are weaker physically than men. This is not a statement of superiority of men or emotional or spiritual weakness of women. In fact, the very next verse goes on to say that women are the coheirs of grace. Peter had talked about our inheritance as believers back in 1 Peter 1:4, and now reminds men that women and men are equal before God (Galatians 3:28). Men and women have been given equal and yet distinct roles, but above all we are called to proclaim the gospel with our lives and be disciples of Jesus.

In what ways can our conduct be just as important as our words, specifically with those closest to us?

What things are people tempted to find value in instead of in Christ?

As a believer in Christ, where should we find our worth and identity?

Read Matthew 11:28–30, Matthew 5:2–12, and Galatians 5:22–23, and note some of the characteristics with which we should adorn ourselves with.

BUT YOU ARE A
CHOSEN RACE, A *ROYAL*
PRIESTHOOD, A *HOLY*
NATION, A PEOPLE FOR
HIS POSSESSION, SO THAT
YOU MAY PROCLAIM THE
PRAISES OF THE ONE
WHO CALLED YOU *OUT*
OF DARKNESS INTO HIS
MARVELOUS LIGHT.

—

1 PETER 2:9

WEEK THREE *reflection*

— 1 Peter 2:9 – 3:7 —

Paraphrase the passage from this week.

What did you observe from this week's text about God and His character?

What does the passage teach about the condition of mankind and about yourself?

How does this passage point to the gospel?

How should you respond to this passage? What is the personal application?

What specific action steps can you take this week to apply the passage?

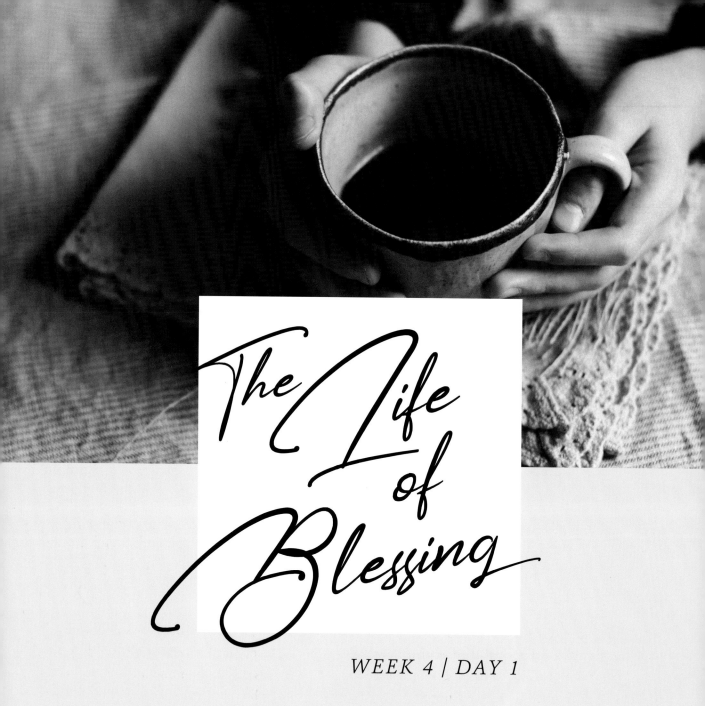

The Life of Blessing

The cares of this life cannot steal away the life of blessing. This is the message of the book of 1 Peter. Our joy is not dependent on our circumstances. Our hope is not hinged to this world. Our joy and our hope are intrinsically tied to the work of Christ for us and to our union with Him. Peter has spent time teaching about specific situations and how the believer should respond in a hostile world, and now Peter gives general instruction for how we should live as elect exiles. He speaks to the collective church and exhorts them to display Christlikeness in their character.

He begins with a call to unity. It is a reminder that though as believers we may have differences, we have the same hope and have received the same grace. Philippians 2:1-11 calls for our unity as well, and here it is directly related to us having the mind of Christ. Several of the other traits listed here in 1 Peter are listed in the Philippians passage as well. Believers should be unified because we have been brought into the family of God. We have been united to Christ and united to each other.

Next is a call to sympathy. This is the call of Romans 12:15. It is a reminder to us to rejoice with those who rejoice and mourn with those who mourn. It is a call to enter into the suffering of others and bear the burdens of one another. Peter then speaks of brotherly love. This is a tender love of friendship. It is a reminder that as believers we do not merely love each other because we are commanded to do so — we love each other because we have friendship that has been made rich through Christ. The love of Christians for one another should not be rivaled. Compassion or having a tender heart comes next. This is a compassion that flows from our inner beings. The word here is used to represent our "guts" or our "bowels." This is a deep love that moves within us to care for each other as Christ has cared for us and lavished us in His grace and compassion (Ephesians 4:32). We are called to be like Him.

Humility is the last on the list, and yet it is a trait that binds the rest of these commands together. When we lack humility, the Christian life becomes an impossible task of trying to live in our own strength. Humility is the glue that binds these traits together. A lack of humility shows that we do not fully understand the gospel. The gospel humbles us. It reminds us of our weakness. Humility is a gift to us because it reminds us that our weakness is a conduit for God's matchless grace. His grace breaks down our pride and flows through our weakness. We can be assured

that Peter felt the depth of these words as he wrote them. He had once in pride declared that he would never deny Jesus (Mark 14:26-31) and had wept over his sin when he had done just what he said he would never do (Mark 14:66-72). Peter knew with confidence the grace of God in his own life, and he wrote with conviction and from a heart that had been transformed with resurrection hope.

The life to which we are called is upside-down. It is one in which we do not retaliate against those who hurt us. It is one in which we are commanded to love our enemies and pray for those who persecute us (Matthew 5:44). This is our calling to bless and to live a life of blessing. Nothing can take away the blessing that we have because of Jesus. Our life here on earth is overflowing with His abundant blessing, and no trials, or suffering, or persecution can take that away because it is tied to Christ who is within us. Our life is a gift of His grace, and if we were to die it would be gain (Philippians 1:21). Peter quotes from Psalm 34:12-16 which is the same passage that he quoted from in 1 Peter 2:3. The Psalm speaks again of the blessed life to which we are called. We do not do good to earn these blessings—we live as a response to the grace we have already received. And whatever we face, whether suffering or abundance, we can be sure that His eyes are upon us.

Look up the words below from verse eight in a dictionary or lexicon,
and write their meanings below.

Unity:

Sympathy:

Love:

Compassion:

Humility:

Read Philippians 2:1–11, and list how Jesus is an example of these traits to us below.

Which one of these traits need to be cultivated in your life right now?
How can you do that?

From these verses what do you understand our calling to be as believers?

DEVOTED
TO GOOD
—

WEEK 4 | DAY 2

Who can harm us when God's eyes are upon us? Peter begins to speak again about Christian suffering, and he encourages us to trust the Lord and fear Him alone. The question at the start of verse 13 is directly connected to what Peter has just quoted from Psalm 34. We know that the eyes of the Lord are on His people. We know that God hears our prayer. We know that He is with us. So, what will we fear? Though it is true that as believers we will face opposition, there is nothing that can have any eternal impact. We are safe in His care. If God is for us, there is nothing that can ever come against us (Romans 8:31, Psalm 56:4, Psalm 118:6). And as the children of God, united with Christ, we know that God is for us. As we are zealous or devoted to what is good, we rest in God's care.

Even if we suffer for the sake of righteousness, Peter tells us that we will be blessed. These words echo the upside-down kingdom language of the Sermon on the Mount. Jesus declared in Matthew 5:10-12 that those persecuted for righteousness would inherit the kingdom of heaven and would receive great reward there. Our perspective must be shifted from the temporal to the eternal. But this promise of blessing is not just in the future — it is also right now and right in the middle of the suffering. Suffering is transformed to blessing in the hands of God. There is blessing in suffering because there is blessing in Jesus, and no matter what suffering we may face, we are in Him.

In John 16:33, Jesus spoke to His disciples and reminded them that though they would face tribulation in this world, they could take heart because He has already overcome. This is the message for us as well. We can take heart. He has already overcome. He has already won the battle. We press on in this battle, but the victory has already been secured. So, Peter tells us to not fear but instead to exalt Christ as Lord. Peter is quoting Isaiah 8:12-13 here, and he clarifies the Old Testament passage by reminding us that Jesus is the Lord. We are free from fear because we fear God alone. We can worship in the waiting and sing through suffering because Jesus has already overcome. When we remember that Christ is Lord, our fears subside. What can we fear? There is nothing that can harm us. Even death has no power over us. We are His, and there is no surer place to be than in His care. The fear of the Lord quiets all other fears.

We can proclaim the hope of the gospel with boldness because this hope is not wishful thinking but confident expectation. We proclaim the truth of the gospel, and we proclaim our own testimony of gospel-transformation. We should be humble and bold — bold in proclaiming

the message and humble in declaring it. The gospel should fill us with humble gratitude for all Christ has done for us, and it should embolden us to herald the truth to everyone we encounter. 1 Peter 1:13 reminded us of what our attitude should be as we live in this world as elect exiles. We should be prepared for action with our hope set fully and without wavering on Jesus alone. Our temporary sufferings are no match for His eternal grace.

Suffering will come. Trials will come. But God is already here. He will not leave us when they come but will walk with us every step of the way. We do not need to vindicate ourselves or fight back against those that would do evil against us. We can trust our reputations to God. We can trust our life in His hands. We can set our hearts on the things above and live heaven-focused lives here on earth through His power. We can live humbly and boldly. We can suffer as He suffered. We can declare the message of gospel-hope to the world around us. But we can do none of this on our own. We can do these things only because He is in us, and He is with us. With our lives and with our words we can declare the gospel and point others to the hope that has set us free.

Suffering is transformed to blessing in the hands of God.

Suffering and blessing seem like opposites, but in this passage, we learn that in the life of the Christian they can go together. How is this so? How is Jesus our example of this?

What are the things that you fear?

How does Jesus drive away our fears?

How can we be always prepared and ready to explain the hope we have in Jesus? How do we prepare for this?

That He might Bring Us to God

WEEK 4 | DAY 3

Christ suffered for us. Now we suffer for Him. In a world where we face suffering, the suffering of Christ reminds us that we do not suffer in vain. He has suffered before us, but now He reigns victorious. The theme of this passage is that Jesus suffered, but He was also exalted. The suffering of Christ led to His glorification, and the same is true for us. Peter encourages us with the reminder that the suffering we face is temporary, and there is glory coming for the people of God.

Verse 18 shows us Jesus as our example. The preceding verses in 1 Peter 3:13-17 and the entirety of 1 Peter have been telling us that we are exiles in this world, but we are united to Christ. Here we are reminded of why Jesus suffered. He suffered once. There was no longer any need for the continual sacrifices of the Old Testament. Jesus is the once-for-all sacrifice that has brought us near to God (Hebrews 9:24-28). Though we are unrighteous, He is the righteous one that has suffered on our behalf. This verse also tells us the reason for this sacrifice. Christ died for us that He might bring us to God. He died for us. He died so that we would no longer be separated but would instead be united with Christ because of the atoning sacrifice of Jesus.

The remainder of 1 Peter 3 is considered by scholars to be the most difficult passage in the New Testament to interpret. There are a variety of opinions on the interpretation, specifically of verse 19 and what it is referring to. There are three main views of the passage. There is a view that Jesus descended into hell after His crucifixion. This view is brought to mind through a line of the Apostle's Creed that was added after its original writing but assumed to mean simply that Jesus descended into the grave. The wording has caused many to remove this line from modern versions of the creed because this view does not line up with the rest of Scripture. The other two views are the most accepted, and each has its own strengths and questions that it raises. The topic is interesting to study, though not essential to understanding the meaning of the passage. The two main views are listed below and on the following page.

— 1 —

One view is that when the passage speaks of Jesus proclaiming to the spirits, it is speaking of the Spirit of Christ speaking through Noah when he warned those who were alive during the time before the flood but are now passed. Most who hold this view take it in context of 1 Peter 1:11-12 where we learned that the Spirit of Christ moved through the prophets to proclaim the gospel.

The second view is that the passage is speaking of Jesus after His death proclaiming to the demonic spirits His victory over them. This view states that Jesus proclaimed or announced to Satan and his demons that He had won the battle at the cross and had defeated them.

Peter then reminds us of how God rescued Noah and his family on the ark which was a picture of salvation. Noah and his family were exiles in their day, just as believers are today. Noah preached the righteousness of God, just as we do today. Noah was mocked, just as believers are. But God would deliver Noah, and God will surely deliver us as well.

The picture of the deliverance of Noah and his family pointed to salvation, and in the same way baptism for the believer also points to salvation. Peter is not saying that we are saved by baptism, but that baptism reflects that we have been saved through the life, death, and resurrection of Jesus. Our baptism is our proclamation of what God has done in us.

Look to the cross. Look to Jesus. This is the message that Peter brings to us. We must not lose this amid the variety of interpretations. The central theme here is that Jesus is victorious, and because we are in Him, we will be victorious as well. We must lift our gaze to the cross and see the one who has suffered for us. We must be reminded of the gospel-truth that Jesus went to the cross so that we could be brought to God. And in Him we can be confident that victory is sure. He is ruling and reigning, and He will not let us down.

Jesus is the once-for-all sacrifice that has brought us near to God.

How does the suffering of Christ bring us hope and encouragement as we face suffering?

Read Hebrews 9:24–28. How is the once–for–all sacrifice better than the repeated sacrifices of the Old Testament? How does it practically change how we live?

This passage has some challenging parts, but the message is one of hope. Summarize the theme of this section and what Peter is trying to convey to us.

How can we look to the cross each day?

LIVE FOR THE WILL OF GOD

—

WEEK 4 | DAY 4

Because of the atoning work of Jesus on the cross, we can die to sin and live for His will. **Despite** suffering and rejection, our hope is secure in Him. Suffering leads to sanctification. And while in many ways this is true in the life of the believer, its full impact is seen in the reminder that Christ's suffering is what leads us to sanctification. The suffering of Jesus gives us resurrection life. Jesus suffered so that we could die to our sin and live to righteousness (1 Peter 2:24). The gospel changes everything, and it is changing us.

The gospel shifts our gaze to God. It takes our eyes off of ourselves and puts them on Jesus. We no longer live for the things of this world, and we no longer chase after our own empty desires. We seek the will of God. As the gospel floods our life we come to realize that God's plan is perfect and high above our own feeble desires. And even if that plan involves suffering, we know that God will only give us what is good for us. Our greatest goal is to know God, and we submit every other dream and goal to that great desire. The desires of our hearts are safe in the hands of God. The will of God for His people is always good. It may not make sense from our human perspective, but He always does what is best for us. As we grow in our walk with God we begin to realize that even when things look bad, we can trust Him to bring good from it (Romans 8:28). As believers who are in Christ, God can give us nothing but goodness. So, as we grow in Him we will begin to see that every "yes" and every "no" is saturated with His goodness. It is in the moments when we struggle to trust Him that we can pray the words of Jesus in Luke 22:42, "Not my will, but yours, be done." Our desires may make us happy for a moment, but our surrender will bring true joy that lasts forever.

In the midst of writing about suffering, Peter reminds us that we are a new creation (2 Corinthians 5:17, Ephesians 4:22-24, John 5:24, Galatians 2:20). In salvation we are given new life, and this new life is different than the life that we once lived. We have been united with Christ, not only in His suffering but also in His resurrection. We live in light of the resurrection. Though still strangers and elect exiles in this world, we live with resurrection-power and gospel-hope. We live for something bigger than this moment. We serve a God who is greater than our situation and stronger than our suffering. Our hope is not hypothetical. We preach the gospel to ourselves and remember that the same power that resurrected Jesus from the grave is now in us (Ephesians 1:15-23). The abundant hope of the gospel floods our souls with expectation.

In this world we are exiles, but we are journeying to the Promised Land. At the start of the book of 1 Peter, Peter addressed his audience as elect exiles. He reminded us that this world is not our home, and because of that this world may not understand us. He speaks here of the way that unbelievers live. They follow after their desires in contrast to how he has just told us to seek after the will of God. Because the believer does not live in the same way, persecution may come. The world does not understand us because we are not of this world. In our union with Christ we have been raised to walk in newness of life.

The gospel is our only hope. And it is the only hope of those apart from Christ. Peter reminds us that this is why the gospel must be preached. This is why the good news of Jesus must be proclaimed. He reminds us that it was preached to those who have gone before us and are now dead. Now the message of salvation continues to be preached because it is our hope. Even death cannot harm the believer who has been given not only a new life but a new life that is eternal. We walk this life as exiles, but we are not without hope. The suffering of this life is temporary and fleeting (2 Corinthians 4:17-18). The persecution of the world will give way to a heavenly reward (Matthew 5:10-11). In this world we will have tribulation, but we can take heart because our God has already overcome (John 16:33). Take heart. He has overcome.

How does the gospel shift our gaze off of ourselves and on to Christ?
Is this something that happens once or something that must happen repeatedly?

What dreams and desires do you need to submit to His will?

How does walking with God grow our trust in God's faithfulness?

Read 2 Corinthians 4:17–18 and Matthew 5:10–11. What do these verses tell us about our trials and persecution? How do they give us hope?

Stewards of Grace

WEEK 4 | DAY 5

Read
1 PETER 4:7-11

We are gifted by God to serve God. This is the message that 1 Peter brings, and it is a timely reminder for us today. Peter writes these words after just telling us to pursue the will of God and stand out from the world around us. Now He is going to tell us how we should live and specifically how we should relate to the covenant community of God. His overarching message to us is that we should glorify God in all things because all glory is His.

The passage begins by telling us that the end is near. This could catch us off guard since we know that it was written 2,000 years ago. We do not know the day of Christ's return, but we do know that we are in the last phase of God's plan and that in that sense the end is near. It is the next event on God's theological timeline. What a comfort to us to see Peter's perspective on the end. There is no doom and gloom here but instead a reminder of God's glory and an exhortation to godliness. As believers, we await the coming of Christ with joy, and know that whether we see Him because of death or because of His return we will one day rejoice in the presence of His glory.

Now things get practical. Because we know that the end is near, we are commanded to live a certain way. Peter is reminding us what Paul taught in Colossians 3:2, that we should set our minds on things above, not on the things of the world. We are commanded to be alert and sober-minded. We are commanded to think clearly so that we can pray. Peter wants us to remember that this world is not our home; it is another reminder that we are the elect exiles. We are God's people here on this earth for just a short time, so we need to make the most of our time here. We need to live for what matters.

As we are told how we should live, a special focus is given to gospel-centered community. We are being told how to interact with the people of God. In verse 8, we are told that above all we must earnestly or constantly love each other. This deep and abiding love will cover a multitude of sins. Peter is referencing Proverbs 10:12 and reminding us that as loving and forgiving believers we are able to stay on mission and not be distracted by unforgiveness and bitterness. Perhaps the words were a reminder to Peter of the time that he had asked Jesus how many times he should forgive. He wanted something quantifiable, but Jesus wanted him to remember that we forgive because we have been forgiven (Matthew 18:21-35). It is true that Christians are to love everyone including our enemies, but Peter puts a special focus here on love within the church. Just because the church is comprised of the people of God does not mean that we will not hurt one another. Peter anticipates that fact and tells us how we should treat each other.

We are encouraged to show hospitality to one another without complaining and to use our gifts to serve each other. We are told that we are to be stewards of God's varied grace. The word here that is translated as "varied" has the idea of "diversity" and "various." He is telling us that we each have been gifted with unique and various strengths in order to serve God. In 1 Peter 1:6 we learned that we would face various trials, but now we are encouraged to know that we have also been graciously gifted with a variety of gifts in order to serve the Lord. He is referring to what is often called spiritual gifts and telling us that there are gifts of all different kinds, and each one is for the glory of God and the service of the church. Your abilities are not an accident, and your giftings are not happenstance. You have been gifted by God to serve and glorify God.

This will look different in each person, and that is why Peter uses the term "varied." He breaks it down for us into two main categories here by addressing those who speak and those who serve. But whether speaking or serving, we must do these through the power of God and to the glory of God. Our areas of service and ministry may look different from one another in the body of Christ, but each one is just as important and valuable. The calling of your pastor and the need for him to proclaim the Word through God's power is no different than the need for those in the nursery to serve through God's strength and for His glory. Whether teaching or opening our home in hospitality, leading from the stage or praying behind the scenes, every person is needed in the church. The exciting and the mundane together are an offering of worship to our Savior.

The passage ends with a doxology because our service should lead us to worship. We have been given gifts of grace, and now we pour them out at the feet of the One who has given everything for us.

Soli Deo Gloria

To the glory of God alone

How is Peter's perspective on the end times different than other perspectives you have heard?

How would being alert and sober-minded change the way that we pray?

List out the things believers are commanded to do in these verses.

How has God gifted you in ways that you can serve God's people?

FINALLY, ALL OF
YOU BE *LIKE-MINDED*
AND *SYMPATHETIC*,
LOVE ONE ANOTHER,
AND BE
COMPASSIONATE
AND *HUMBLE*

—

1 PETER 3:8

WEEK FOUR *reflection*

— 1 Peter 3:8 — 4:11 —

Paraphrase the passage from this week.

What did you observe from this week's text about God and His character?

What does the passage teach about the condition of mankind and about yourself?

How does this passage point to the gospel?

How should you respond to this passage? What is the personal application?

What specific action steps can you take this week to apply the passage?

REJOICE IN SUFFERING

—

WEEK 5 | DAY 1

Do not be surprised by suffering. Trials will come, and we can rejoice right in their midst. This message is upside-down to us. It reminds us of the upside-down kingdom that Jesus spoke of (Matthew 5-7). In the kingdom of God, things are not always what you would expect, and that is the beauty of following Jesus. His ways are higher than our ways, and we can trust Him to always do what is right. As Peter prepares to close the book of 1 Peter, he is circling back to many of the concepts that we have already discussed. Like a good teacher, he is reminding us of his most important points. As exiles in this world, we will face suffering, and we shouldn't be surprised. Even in suffering, the light of God's grace pierces through the darkness.

Suffering and trials take us by surprise. They come without warning and sometimes leave us wondering why bad things are happening when we have been faithfully pursuing the Lord. Yet Scripture flips this notion around. We are reminded that Jesus is our example. He is the one who we follow, and we are His disciples. We look to the pattern of His life, and as His people we can expect the pattern of our own life to be the same as we follow after Him. He suffered, but He then was glorified. Here we see that we rejoice now even though we suffer because someday we will rejoice in glory. So, we claim our sufferings as promises of that living hope. We view our life from God's perspective.

The life of blessing is not separated from a life of suffering. Peter references the Sermon on the Mount here when he says that if we are insulted for the name of Christ we are blessed (Matthew 5:10-12). He then tells us that the Spirit of glory and of God rests upon us. God's presence is often felt strongest in suffering. We feel God's comfort in our weakness. We recognize our need for the covenant community of the church. Our darkest days draw us into the comfort of His arms.

We must live righteously through suffering. Peter reminds us that we must not suffer for sin but for the sake of righteousness. In our suffering for Christ we must take on the posture of the apostle Paul in the book of Romans when he declared that he was not ashamed of the gospel (Romans 1:16-17). We can rejoice in the honor of being called to suffer in His name. We must reject sin and live righteously. Verse 18 speaks of the difficulty of being saved. It is not speaking here of any form of uncertainty in our salvation. Instead he is telling us that though the salvation of believers is assured, the road toward final victory is often a difficult one. We cling to the certain hope of our salvation while we walk through the wilderness of suffering.

The chapter ends with a call to those who will suffer and face trials. The call is for us to entrust our souls to our creator while we continue to serve Him. In 1 Peter 2:23, we saw Jesus as our example of entrusting Himself through suffering to the One who judges justly. Now we are reminded to entrust ourselves to the Lord who is the faithful creator. If He cares for all of creation, He can certainly care for us. We can trust Him. He is trustworthy. Jesus is our example, and we have been united with Christ. We face our suffering with His example before us, Christ in us, and the reminder that glory is to come. The outcome is certain, but the path is not always easy. Yet through this wilderness journey His grace pours down on us as a reminder that He is going with us every step of the way. The call to us is this: Be ready for trials, and rejoice in those trials. Live righteously, and then run to Jesus.

———

That is the beauty of following Jesus.
His ways are higher than our ways, and we can
trust Him to always do what is right.

Why should suffering not surprise us as believers?

Read 1 Peter 4:14 and Matthew 5:10–12. What is upside-down about these verses?

Have you ever experienced God's presence and blessing right in the midst of suffering and trials?

How can we practically entrust our souls to the Lord?

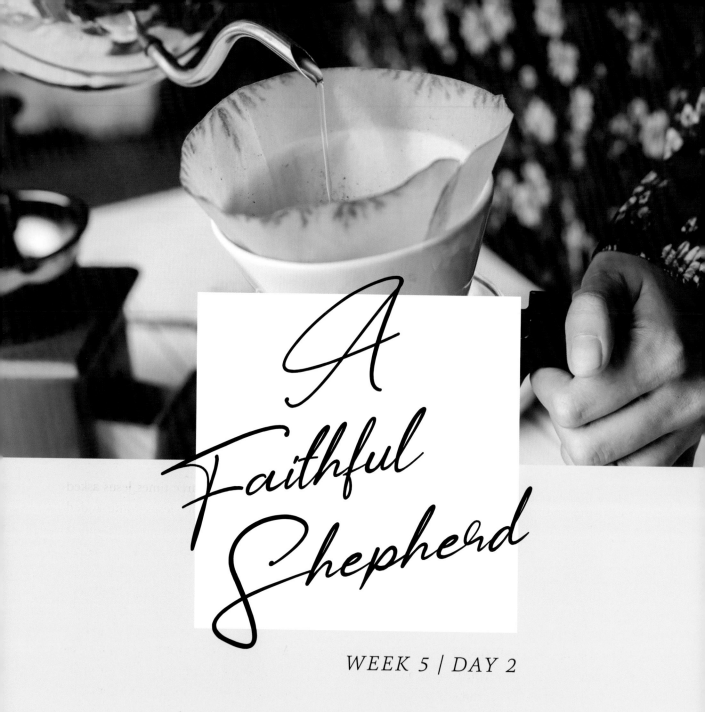

A Faithful Shepherd

WEEK 5 | DAY 2

Read
1 PETER 5:1-5

We have come to the last chapter of 1 Peter. Peter continues to review some of the major themes of the book, and in this section, he introduces us to instructions for one more group of people. These are the elders of the church. Peter speaks to the elders as a fellow elder and a witness to Christ's suffering and as one who looks forward to the glory to come. Peter exemplifies humility as he does not elevate himself above his audience and remind them of who he is. Instead of pointing to himself, he points to Christ. Instead of seeking after his own glory, he does all for the glory of God. This is a reminder to us of how we should live, and it is a shining example to the church leaders who he is speaking to of how to be a servant-leader.

Peter's message to the elders of the church is to shepherd the people of God. Though Peter will go on to tell these elders some of the things that they should do and some of the things that they should not do, this word "shepherd" is overflowing with implications for how the elders should lead. But we cannot begin to look at those things without first recognizing the weight of the words coming from Peter. Peter had once denied even knowing Jesus, but after the resurrection he sat over breakfast with Jesus and found hope and restoration. Three times Jesus asked Peter if he loved Him, and three times after Peter responded that he did, Jesus commanded Peter to feed His sheep (John 21:15-19). Peter had been commanded by the Good Shepherd to be a shepherd to the people of God (John 10:14-18). That is exactly what Peter would go on to do. Even through the words of this short letter, Peter fulfills the call of God on His life to shepherd God's people. Though once a failure, Peter now was a shepherd following in the footsteps of his Great Shepherd.

The concept of the shepherd is no stranger to Scripture. Moses and David were both named as shepherds of God's people (Isaiah 63:11, 2 Samuel 5:2). God is called our shepherd throughout the Scriptures, including in Psalm 23 that beautifully describes the Lord as our Shepherd. And even here in 1 Peter we were reminded that Jesus is the Shepherd and Overseer of our souls (1 Peter 2:25). The call of the shepherd is to feed, protect, and guide the sheep. Jesus is our ultimate Shepherd, and He has graciously called servant-leaders to shepherd us as well. Jesus who is our Shepherd walks before us as our example of an elect exile. He shows us the path of suffering that leads to glory. And He gives us elders to help lead the path on this earth.

The picture of the elder and shepherd is a beautiful one. Yet, this picture does not take for granted the fact that there will be some who abuse the role that they are in. Peter speaks directly to

some of the common issues faced by those in leadership. He speaks to the possibility of a leader compelled to lead and says that elders should be willing leaders. He speaks to the possibility of leaders who serve for money instead of with godly motives, and he tells us that elders should be eager leaders serving for the glory of Christ and not financial gain. And he speaks to the possibility of abuse of power and reminds leaders that they are to be humble leaders who serve as examples of what it means to follow Jesus. Leaders will let us down. Churches may let us down, but we must look to Jesus above all.

The reward of leaders following Jesus is that they will receive the crown of glory. This is again, not a crown of gold, but the victor's wreath. Throughout this entire letter, Peter has been showing us how we will face suffering in this world, but there is glory coming (1 Peter 1:11, 13, 21, 4:13, 5:1, 10). He gives us that same picture here. On this earth we are called to endure, but there is coming a day when we will share in the glory of Christ. For now, we live in hope, but there is coming a day when hope will give way to every promise fulfilled.

The church is made up of imperfect people, and that is precisely the reason that we need Jesus. Yet as we grow in our love for Jesus, we also grow in love for the things that He loves. Jesus loves the church, and we should as well. In the church, we can submit to those who have gone before us and who seek to lead us to know God more, and we can lead those who are spiritually younger than us. We look forward to the day when all suffering will be erased, and we will worship our Shepherd and King forever.

Read John 21:15–19. How does this passage give you insight into Peter and what he would have meant when he spoke of church leaders as shepherds?

In what ways is God our Shepherd?

In what ways are church leaders to be our shepherds?

Read 1 Peter 1:11, 13, 21, 4:13, 5:1, and 10. Paraphrase the theme that you see recurring in all of these verses from 1 Peter.

ALL YOUR ANXIETY

—

WEEK 5 | DAY 3

Read

1 PETER 5:5-7

Clothe yourselves with humility. This is the command that we are given as Peter continues in the second half of verse five. The Greek here is to literally tie or gird something around your waist. The word was typically used of a servant tying an apron around his or her waist to serve. We are told that the thing that should be tied around us is humility itself. It seems Peter is referencing a very important moment in his own life by using these words and recalling the night when Jesus Himself tied a towel around His waist and knelt down to wash the feet of the disciples including the feet of Peter (John 13:1-20). Peter pushed against Jesus washing His feet because he knew that this was backwards. But Jesus was not afraid to get low. He came as a servant, and He faced suffering. Jesus came to teach us that the kingdom of God is an upside-down kingdom and that humility comes before exaltation.

Peter has been teaching us this message for all of 1 Peter. He has been reminding us that we follow the example of Jesus. In the book of Philippians, Paul tells us that we are to have the same mind of Christ (Philippians 2:1-11). We are to be humble as Jesus was humble. There is not one Christian who is exempt from this call to humility. It is the call of every disciple because it is the call of our Savior. Peter quotes Proverbs 3:34 that is also quoted in James 4:6 and reminds us that though God is opposing the proud, He pours out grace for the humble. We are called to humble ourselves under the mighty hand of God. Is there any better place to be than in His hand? This is the place of security. This is the place where our anxieties melt away. This is the place of protection as we journey as exiles. We humble ourselves knowing that He will exalt us at just the right time. God is never late, and we can trust that He will not be late for us. He came to save us at just the right time, even though we were yet sinners (Romans 5:6, Galatians 4:4). Peter draws from the words of Psalm 55:22 which goes on to tell us that the Lord will never allow the righteous to be moved. We are safe to rest our past, present, and future in the hands of the Lord. He will be faithful to us.

Immediately after the call to humility before God comes the command to cast our anxieties on Him — it is through the humble recognition of our need for Him that we loosen our grip on the worries we clench in our hands. The word for "cast" here has the idea of "to throw them." We must throw them to Jesus and not pick them up again. Pride multiplies our cares as we think that everything depends on us, but humility frees us from the anxieties that weigh us down as we realize that the cross has lifted our burdens and placed them on Jesus. Humility allows us to be reminded that we are not God, and we do not need to control our situation. The reminder of our need frees us to find rest from the worries of our hearts.

Jesus calls us to come to Him. He calls us to come and find rest. In Matthew 11:27-30, Jesus tells us to come to Him and find rest. In the greater context of this verse, we see the disciples facing difficult circumstances, and then in these verses Jesus gives them the prerequisite for that rest. In order to know rest and freedom from our anxiety, we must know Jesus. There is no rest apart from Jesus. This isn't just relaxation—it is rest for our souls. Jesus is rest for our weary souls. And even here in this passage, we see that our rest is tied to us learning the humility of Christ. There is rest to be found in waiting on the Lord and surrendering to His control. There is rest and freedom from anxiety to be found in sitting at the feet of Jesus and learning from Him. Mary and Martha are two women that demonstrated this for us. Martha was concerned about all of the things that needed to be done, and she was overwhelmed with the anxiety of her day. She wanted to have it all together, but Mary sat at the feet of Jesus. Mary learned from Him and found rest (Luke 10:38-42). May we be women who choose to humble ourselves and sit at the feet of Jesus. May we be women who set aside "all of the things," so that we can focus on the most important thing—the most important One.

Casting our anxieties and cares on Jesus does not mean that they disappear—it means they are no longer our burden to bear. It means the things that once weighed us down are now carried by Him. Casting our anxieties on Him doesn't negate the weight of our burdens—it confirms it. We have burdens too heavy for us to bear, but we have a God who is strong enough to bear them for us. We do not need to search for a way to make our worries go away but for somewhere to place them. Getting it all together is not the solution for our anxieties. The solution is getting it all on Jesus.

———

Is there any better place to be than in His hand?

This is the place of security.
This is the place where our anxieties melt away.

How can humility ease our anxiety?

Read Matthew 11:28–30. What do these verses tell us about Jesus and what He does and about us and what we are called to do?

Read Luke 10:38–42. How do these verses remind you about the importance of choosing the most important things? What are the most important things that you need to choose today?

What burdens do you need to cast or throw on Jesus today?
Take time to pray about the burdens and anxieties that are weighing on you.

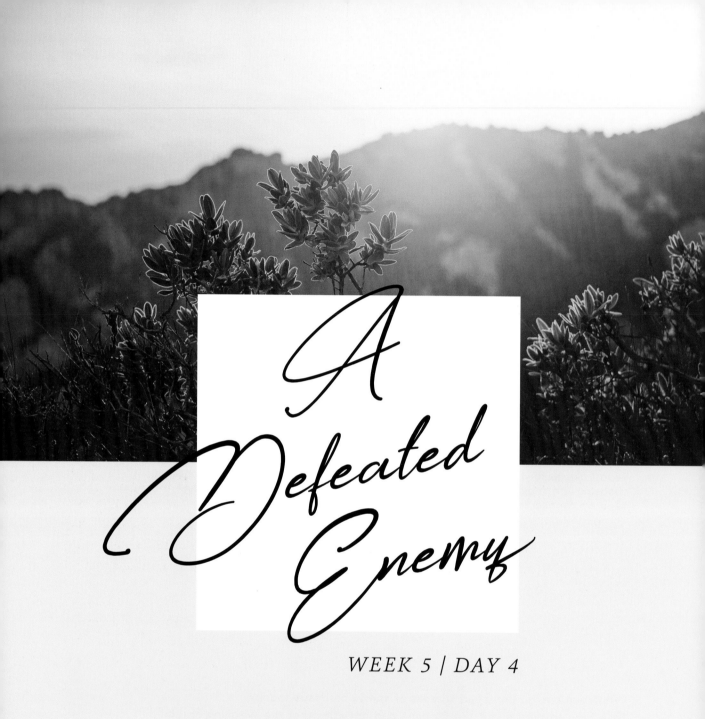

A Defeated Enemy

WEEK 5 | DAY 4

Read

1 PETER 5:8-9

Pay attention!!! Peter wants us to be on alert. He doesn't want us to get complacent or distracted. He refreshes our memories with commands that he has already given us in this letter. He wants us to be sober-minded and alert or watchful. He wants us to be aware of what is going on. But this time, he digs a little deeper and tells us why we need to be paying attention. We need to pay attention because there is an enemy out to get us.

This enemy is cunning and crafty. He is our adversary the devil. Our greatest enemy is Satan himself. Here the word "adversary" is a legal term. Satan is our accuser. He is the prosecutor against us. We see a picture of this in Job 1:6-12 and Job 2:1-6. In his cunning, crafty, and sinful way, Satan prowls the earth seeking to destroy and studying the weaknesses of men. His desire is to thwart the plan of God, but though he may experience what seems like small victories, he is destined for defeat.

The word "devil" that is used in these verses could be translated as "deceiver," and it is a glimpse into one of the most prominent tactics in our enemy's playbook. He seeks to deceive us. He wants to make us question God and His goodness to us just as he did to Eve in the garden (Genesis 3:1). He wants to make us wonder if God is holding out on us. He wants to make us think that he isn't a big deal or even that he doesn't exist. The devil delights in our sin. He celebrates our anxieties. He laughs at our sorrows. He is the opposite of everything that God is. He is real, and he is deplorable, but he will not be victorious.

The image of the roaring lion goes far deeper than we would probably realize at first glance. For the early Christians who would have read this, the image that would have been brought to mind was not that of a zoo or a children's book. The picture of a lion would have reminded them of the Roman Colosseum and the lions that would kill and destroy the Christians who were thrown to the lions while a laughing crowd looked on. The image is a sober realization of the battle that we are in.

In Ephesians 6:11-20, Paul describes for us the armor of God. He tells us that we are in a spiritual battle and that we need spiritual armor to be victorious in battle. He tells us to put on this armor so that we can stand against the schemes of the devil. He reminds us that we do not wrestle against flesh and blood, but instead we battle the unseen forces of evil. Peter is reminding us of this same truth. Peter has just written for chapters about the suffering and trials

that come to those who stand for the Lord, and now he takes a moment to pause and remind us that our true enemy is not the people who we can see, but the one who we cannot see. Our enemy is sin and the one who seeks to tempt us to sin. Camouflaged behind so many of our troubles lies a cunning enemy.

We are commanded to resist him. We submit to God. We submit to one another. We submit to those in authority over us. But when it comes to our enemy, we resist with everything we have. In our resisting we are told to be firm in our faith — solid and unmovable like a rock. Perhaps it reminded Peter of the time that Jesus had called him a rock (Matthew 16:13-20). Peter knew that with Jesus as our chief cornerstone, we were being called to be living stones (1 Peter 2:4-12), and that we must stand firm in the sold rock of our faith that compels us to live in hope. Peter ends verse 9 by reminding us that we are not alone. The things that we face are the things that believers through all the ages have faced before us. In salvation we are united to Christ, but we are also united to the church, and we find comfort in each other (2 Corinthians 1:3-5). We are stronger together.

The good news is that though we have a very real enemy, he is already defeated. Though we still battle against sin, the cross has already defeated sin and Satan. We now wait for the day when all will be restored, and we will see the full completion of that defeat. We press on and stand firm in the knowledge that though we have a powerful enemy, we have a God who is so much stronger.

In these verses we are commanded to be sober-minded and alert or watchful. What would be the opposite of this?

Look up the word "resist," and write the definition below.

Read Ephesians 6:11-20. What insight do you find in these verses about how to resist our enemy?

How does the gospel give us comfort that our enemy is already defeated?

STAND IN HIS GRACE

—

WEEK 5 | DAY 5

In a world of suffering we rest in the sovereign and sufficient grace of God. We live in hope because of our living hope. We cling to the Word of God that sustains us. We find comfort in our calling as His chosen people. This is what we have learned in the book of 1 Peter.

As Peter closes the book, he reminds us that though in this world we will suffer, it is only for a little while. Though our trials seem long, they are just a moment compared to what God has for His people. Suffering is temporary, but His grace is not. His grace is everlasting and stunning. It overflows in our moments of sorrow and comforts us in our need. It brings joy right in the midst of our struggles. Someday we will look back on the momentary suffering of our lives and be reminded that even then He was working. He will use every trial and every tear to refine us. He will take every testing and every trouble, and He will redeem them.

And then when our trials are passed, the God of grace—the One who called us to be His own will be the one to restore us. He will restore us. He will establish or confirm us. He will strengthen us. He will support us. He will not let us wait a moment too long. He will not let us cry one tear too many. He will use every ounce of our sorrow for our good. He will use every weakness to remind us of His strength.

He has called us to an eternal glory. He has called us to an inheritance that this world cannot steal away. He has called us to His glory. He has called us to be united with Jesus. Peter has shown us that for now we are united with Him in suffering, but there is coming a day when we will also be united with Him in glory. This is a firm and secure promise. Paul speaks in Romans 8:29-30 of many of the same themes that we have seen in 1 Peter. The same God that called us and knew us before time began will conform us to the image of Jesus. He has saved us, and He will sustain us. And those who He has justified, He has glorified. Paul affirms the surety of this hope by using the past tense. Though we wait for its complete fulfillment, it is as good as done. Jesus has already paid the price on the cross. We are already united with Him if we are His children. And there will be a day when we will be glorified, and every sorrow will vanish. This is our hope. This is our confident expectation. God will do what He has promised. Peter can't stop from bursting into praise in verse 11 at the reality of the sure faithfulness of God, and we should do the same.

Peter closes his letter with final greetings and the mention of those who have been his faithful ministry partners. He mentions for us Silvanus (or Silus) and Mark. And then he mentions Babylon. At this point in history the city of Babylon had already been destroyed, but this reference is a symbolic reference that takes us all the way back to the beginning of the book. At the start of 1 Peter, Peter called the believers the elect exiles. And here he references the capital city of the exile, and it is just one more reminder that the people of God are the new exiled people of God. Here Babylon is symbolic of Rome and the chosen in Babylon a symbol of the church of Rome.

Peter wrote this letter to exhort us. He wrote to encourage us. He wrote to declare or testify to the grace of God. And now he ends by telling us to stand firm in that amazing grace. The grace of God is our anchor in this storm-tossed life. The grace of God enables us to stand firm in Him who is our strong foundation. The grace of God will carry us to glory.

A salutation of peace is the most fitting ending to this book. Jesus who is our peace (Ephesians 2:14) left this earth with a similar message. He left us with peace (John 14:27). And the peace that Jesus gives, this world cannot take away. There is peace in Christ no matter what life brings. And we as His people are in Christ. We have union with Him. And though we share for this moment in His sufferings, there is coming a day when every sorrow will be erased, and we will share in glory beyond our imagination (2 Corinthians 4:16-18). So, for now we fix our hearts on the eternal and the eternal way. We rest in His faithfulness, and we stand in His grace.

————

He has called us
To an eternal glory
To an inheritance that this world cannot steal away
To His glory
To be united with Jesus.

What comfort do you find in the truth that our suffering is temporary?

From a lexicon, concordance, or English dictionary define the four things that verse 10 tells us that God will do.

How can you stand firm in the grace of God?

Summarize the message of 1 Peter.

INSTEAD, *REJOICE*
AS YOU *SHARE IN THE*
SUFFERINGS OF CHRIST,
SO THAT YOU MAY ALSO
REJOICE WITH GREAT
JOY WHEN HIS GLORY
IS REVEALED.

—

1 PETER 4:13

WEEK FIVE *reflection*

— 1 Peter 4:12 — 5:14 —

Paraphrase the passage from this week.

What did you observe from this week's text about God and His character?

What does the passage teach about the condition of mankind and about yourself?

How does this passage point to the gospel?

How should you respond to this passage? What is the personal application?

What specific action steps can you take this week to apply the passage?

TIMELINE
OF EVENTS

Leading up to the dispersion of Exiles.
i.e. Nero's rule & consequences of that rule within Rome

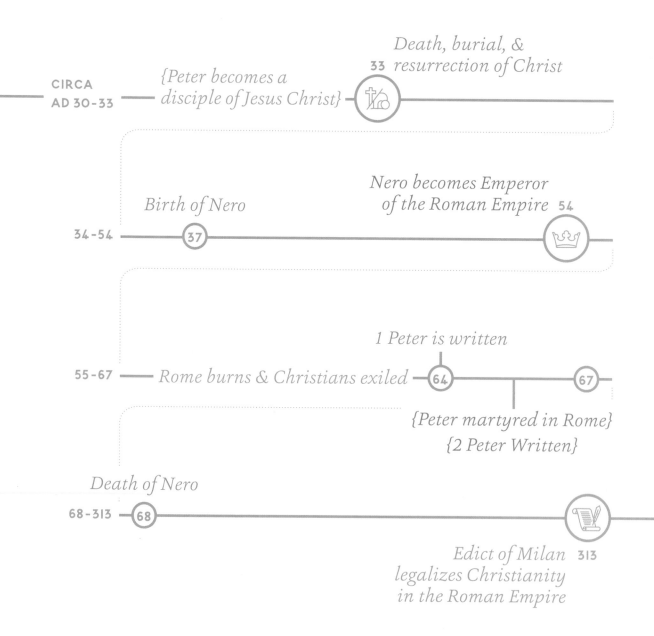

Death, burial, &
33 *resurrection of Christ*

CIRCA
AD 30-33 — *{Peter becomes a disciple of Jesus Christ}*

Nero becomes Emperor
of the Roman Empire **54**

Birth of Nero

34-54 — **37**

1 Peter is written

55-67 — Rome burns & Christians exiled — **64** — **67**

{Peter martyred in Rome}
{2 Peter Written}

Death of Nero

68-313 — **68**

Edict of Milan **313**
legalizes Christianity
in the Roman Empire

THE EXILES' DISPERSION

This map shows the areas where the exiles
and recipients of this letter lived.

EXILES IN SCRIPTURE

—

& how they relate to the exiles in 1 Peter.

THE EXILES OF 1 PETER

The first letter that Peter wrote is addressed to the "chosen exiles dispersed abroad in Pontus, Galatia, Cappadocia, Asia, and Bithynia." Exiles are individuals who have been forced out of their homeland, into a foreign land, usually because of political or religious alignment, and this idea is pretty prominent in the Bible, with the word being used 105 times throughout Scripture. The people Peter wrote to were believers who had been forcibly removed by decree of Emperor Nero from their homes in Rome. This wasn't the first case of exile that our Bibles tell us about, though.

THE FIRST EXILES

In Genesis 3:23-24, we see that because of Adam and Eve's disobedience, they are exiled from the perfect garden that they once inhabited. They were removed, by God, from their home because of their sin. In 2 Kings 17:23, Israel is exiled because of their disobedience toward God's statutes, and in 2 Kings 25:21 we see that Judah was exiled from the land that God gave them because of their rebellion against Him. One aspect of what God taught Israel and Judah through their exile is this: *on earth, we will always long for home and peace, but we are not guaranteed these securities in this life but only in the life to come.*

EXILES AND THE GOSPELS

Throughout the Gospels of Matthew, Mark, Luke, and John, we see Jesus beckoning to those who have been "exiled" and are without home or any sense of belonging. Lepers, adulterers, the blind, the lame, and the beggars all are invited into His divine fold. Through these instances, we are allowed to see something significant—home, security, and belonging is found in Jesus Christ. Peter's letter to the exiles is significant to us today, not necessarily because we've been political or religious exiles, but because this world is not our home. We reside as aliens in this world, sojourners awaiting their permanent, eternal inheritance. The words of Peter remind us that our fulfilment and joy is only found in Christ and that our true homes are in heaven.

EXILES

—

Individuals who have been forced out of their homeland, into a foreign land, usually because of political or religious alignment.

....

"EXILES" IS SEEN

105 TIMES

throughout Scripture

....

O.T. EXAMPLES

—

Genesis 3:23–24
Adam & Eve

2 Kings 17:23
Israel

2 Kings 25:21
Judah

PETER'S LETTER & US TODAY:

This world is not our home. We reside as aliens in this world, sojourners awaiting their permanent, eternal inheritance.

1 PETER
Old Testament Cross References

Peter is a Jewish Christian, and throughout his first epistle he uses Old Testament language to communicate to the Gentile-Christian exiles about their adoption into the family of God. By expressing Old Testament Jewish concepts, Peter is reminding these Gentile Christians of their new heritage through Christ.

CHOSEN	EXILED	HOLINESS	PASSOVER
+	+	+	+
1 Peter 1:1-2	1 Peter 1:1-2	1 Peter 1:15-16	1 Peter 1:19
Genesis 18:19	Genesis 23:4	Leviticus 19:2	Exodus 12:5

IMPERISHABLE WORD OF GOD	A HOLY TEMPLE, LIVING STONES	ROYAL PRIESTHOOD	A HOLY NATION
+	+	+	+
1 Peter 1:22-25	1 Peter 2:1-8	1 Peter 2:9	1 Peter 2:9
Isaiah 40:6-8	Isaiah 28:16	Exodus 19:5-6	Deut. 26:19
	Psalm 118:22		

GOD'S POSSESSION	WORSHIPERS OF GOD	CALLED FROM DARKNESS	
+	+	+	
1 Peter 2:9	1 Peter 2:9	1 Peter 2:9	
Deut. 14:2	Isaiah 43:21	Isaiah 9:2	

Matthew 4:18-20 *Mark 1:16-17* *Luke 5:1-11*	*Peter, a fisherman, decides to follow Jesus who promised to make them "fishers of men."*
Matthew 8:14-15 *Mark 1:29-31* *Luke 4:38-39*	*Jesus heals Peter's mother-in-law.*
Matt. 10:1-14 *Mark 3:13-19* *Luke 6:12-16*	*Disciples officially called. Jesus gives them authority over unclean spirits, power to heal diseases, and He sends them out to preach that the kingdom of heaven is at hand.*
Matthew 14:28-31	*Peter walks with Jesus on water, but sinks because of doubt.*
Matthew 16:16 *Mark 8:29* *Luke 9:20*	*Peter confesses Jesus as the Christ.*
Matthew 16:18	*Jesus declares His church will be built upon Peter.*
Matthew 16:22-23 *Mark 8:32-33*	*Peter attempts to rebuke Jesus for the foretelling of His death—Jesus calls him Satan.*
Matthew 17:1-13 *Mark 9:2-13* *Luke 9:28-36*	*Peter, James, and John are present at the transfiguration.*
Matthew 17:24-27	*Jesus asks Peter to open the mouth of a fish for taxes.*

Matthew 18:21	*Peter asks how often we ought to forgive.*
Matthew 19:27 *Mark 10:28* *Luke 18:28*	*Peter asks what the disciples will inherit in return for having left everything to follow Him.*
John 13:6-10	*Jesus washes Peter's feet.*
Matthew 26:30-35 *Mark 14:26-31* *Luke 22:31-34* *John 13:36-38*	*Jesus tells Peter that he will deny Him;* *Peter swears he won't.*
Matthew 26:36-46 *Mark 14:33-42* *Luke 22:39-46*	*Peter, James and John are taken to Garden of Gethsemane to pray with Jesus.*
Matthew 26:51-56 *Mark 14:47-52* *Luke 22:50* *John 18:10*	*Peter cuts off the soldier's ear.*
Matthew 26:58 *Mark 14:54*	*Peter secretly watches Jesus before the council.*
Matthew 26:69-75 *Mark 14:66-72* *Luke 22:54-62* *John 18:15-18, 25-27*	*Peter denies Christ three times.*

Luke 24:12 *John 20:2-10*	*Peter runs to the empty tomb.*
Mark 16:12-13	*The resurrected Christ appears to Peter and John.*
John 21:15-19	*Jesus asks Peter to feed His sheep and follow Him.*
Acts 1:12-14	*Peter, along with other disciples, return to Jerusalem after the Ascension of Christ, devoting themselves to prayer with "the women and Mary the mother of Jesus and His brothers."*
Acts 2:14-40	*Peter gives a sermon at Pentecost.*
Acts 3:1-7	*Peter heals the lame beggar.*
Acts 3:11-26	*Peter speaks in Solomon's portico, proclaiming the gospel.*
Acts 4:1-22	*Peter defends healing the beggar before Jewish council.*
Acts 5:18-19	*Peter is jailed for preaching, and is quickly released by an angel of the Lord.*
Acts 10:9-33 *Acts 11:1-18*	*Peter has a vison from God: "do not call common what God has made clean." The gospel is for the Gentiles.*
Acts 12:1-19	*Peter is imprisoned, then rescued by an angel.*
Galatians 2:7-8, 11-14	*Peter becomes a hypocrite, abiding in the Law in his ministry to the Jews.*